The Perfect Speller

THE NO NONSENSE LIBRARY

No Nonsense Reference Guides

The Perfect Speller

No Nonsense Career Guides

Managing Time
No Nonsense Management
How to Choose a Career
How to Re-enter the Workforce
How to Write a Resume
Power Inverviewing
Succeeding With Difficult People

No Nonsense Financial Guides

Making Money With Credit and Credit Cards
Investing in Mutual Funds
Investing in the Stock Market
Investing in Tax Free Bonds
Understanding Investing
Understanding Money Market Funds
Understanding IRA's
Understanding Treasury Bills and Other U.S. Government Securities
Understanding Common Stocks
Understanding Stock Options and Futures Markets
Understanding Social Security
Understanding Insurance
How to Plan and Invest for Your Retirement
Making a Will and Creating Estate Plans
Understanding Condominiums and Co-ops
How to Buy a Home
Understanding Mortgages and Home Equity Loans

No Nonsense Success Guides

No Nonsense Health Guides

No Nonsense Cooking Guides

No Nonsense Parenting Guides

NO NONSENSE REFERENCE GUIDE™

The

Perfect

Speller

Teri Gordon

*This book is dedicated
to my husband, Al.*

Copyright © 1992 by Teri Gordon

Published by Longmeadow Press, 201 High Ridge Road, Stamford, CT 06904. All rights reserved. No part of this book may be reproduced or utilized in any form or by any means, electronic or mechanical, including photocopying, recording or by any information storage and retrieval system, without permission in writing from the Publisher.

Cover design by Nancy Sabato

Library of Congress Cataloging-in-Publication Data

Gordon, Teri.
    No nonsense success guide : the perfect speller / by Teri Gordon. — 1st ed.
        p.   cm.
    Includes index.
    ISBN: 0-681-41796-X : $4.95
    1. English language—Orthography and spelling.   I. Title.
PE1145.2.G66   1992
428.1—dc20

92-39608
CIP

Printed in the United States of America
Second Edition
0 9 8 7 6 5 4 3 2 1

Contents

Preface

This book has been created to help those of you who have difficulty spelling **frequently-used words**.

To some, spelling comes easily; one look and the letters are embedded in their mind, never to be forgotten. To others, their talents lie in other interests.

However, to be able to get along in our ever-more-complex world, reading and writing are an important part of our daily living.

Hopefully, this book will help you master some basics. I have kept grammar to a minimum so that I do not lose your attention.

TERI GORDON
Teacher, Writer, Editor

Helpful Hints

<u>DO NOT BELIEVE EVERYTHING YOU READ IS SPELLED CORRECTLY</u>! Not even if it is in print! Once you learn the correct spelling, do not doubt that <u>your</u> spelling is right. You might even become annoyed when you see misspelled words.

<u>PROPER PRONUNCIATION IS IMPORTANT TO CORRECT SPELLING</u>. If syllables are sloppy or omitted, spelling will be affected. The omission of word endings will produce the same result. Help yourself to spell accurately by saying the word clearly first. Exaggerate pronunciation, if necessary. Avoid carelessness. (Your speech will also be improved.)

<u>WHEN YOU SEE A NEW WORD, NOTICE ANY PECULIAR SPELLING OR EXTRA LETTERS</u>. Try to remember its unusual features. Link it in your mind with a similar word or create your own ''crutch'' for locking it in your memory.

<u>MAKE A LIST OF THE WORDS YOU LOOK UP IN THE DICTIONARY</u>. Write both your spelling and the dictionary spelling. Often the same words will be repeated. Analyze what you consistently do wrong. Learn to spell problem words correctly so you'll never have to look them up again.

<u>AFTER WRITING A WORD CORRECTLY</u>:
Study it for a few moments.
Say it and spell it aloud as you write it five times.
Be sure to pronounce it accurately.

Look at the word again just before bedtime. Say it and spell it once.

If necessary, create your own "crutch". You'll probably never misspell it again. You will have conquered it.

<u>THERE</u> <u>ARE</u> EXCEPTIONS <u>TO</u> SPELLING <u>RULES</u>. Read a word after making any changes. If the new spelling reads awkwardly, it's usually wrong.

<u>ALWAYS REREAD</u> <u>WHAT</u> <u>YOU</u> HAVE <u>WRITTEN</u>. You will catch many slips if you do. Do this even if you are writing words that you know how to spell. Everyone slips up occasionally, especially when writing in a hurry.

How to Use This Book

Words are arranged alphabetically. Locate your problem word. Next to it, you will find some sentences that include this word and one or more which may be similar or related in spelling. These should help you remember the right spelling of your problem word.

Select one sentence that you would be comfortable with and try to recall it whenever you need to spell that word. Below the sentences, you will find a few more words that may be familiar to you. If you feel that this is not enough, see HELPFUL HINTS which begins on page 1.

A small "h" indicates that a word is a homonym. It sounds like another word or words but it differs in meaning. When a word is a homonym, locate it in the homonym section on page 67. There you will find words that sound like your word but may tend to confuse your spelling. Separating these words in your mind will prevent you from substituting the spelling of one for the spelling of another.

To assist you with words not listed, review the Basic Spelling Rules listed in the CONTENTS. These have been kept to a minimum.

A separate section is devoted to words that have an unusual spelling. Reviewing these for only a few minutes will be time well spent.

Words Frequently
Misspelled
(With Spelling Hints)

ACCOMMODATE Acco's M & M's are great on a
date.
To accommodate the accountant, get a new commode.
If you accomplish the work on time, you will accommodate the commissioner.
Hints: access, accede, accord, common, community, commo-
dious

ACCUSTOM A circus group must accustom itself to
each new environment.
It is always difficult to accustom ourselves to a new
bus schedule.
Can he accustom himself to the new trust?
Hints: discus, accuse, locust, bicuspid, excuse, busy,
gusty

ACHIEVE A thief will achieve grief.
Can she achieve a perfect pie?
I believe we can achieve some success.
Hints: sieve, lie, mischievous, relieve, hie, tie, diet, Juliet

ACQUAINT Acquaint yourself with the uses of lacquer.

If you acquire a new appliance, acquaint yourself with
all its parts.

I will acquaint you with the terms of the pact.

Hints: action, accident, react, race, rack, pace, track, Grace

ACQUAINTANCE Act quaint at a distance.
For instance, how did she react to your new acquaintance?
June is an acquaintance, met by accident.
Hints: extract, lacquer, chance, race, pace, prance, dance, pact

ACQUIRE May we acquire access to the room?
Will we acquire a clothes rack soon?
The director must acquire another actor.
Hints: action, react, accident, place, lace, lacquer, racket

ACTUAL An actual race will be a practical solution.
It was an actual fact; ACT I had ended.
A good actor can achieve actual silence from an audience.
Hints: bract, contractual, back, hack, jack, lack, stack, brace

ADVICE (noun) My advice is to serve rice.
"Stay off the ice" is good advice.
It's good advice to avoid lice, mice and vice.
Hints: device, nice, dice, price, jaundice, avarice, spice, strict

ADVISE (verb) Be wise; don't advise.
She may advise you to rise early.
I advise you to be careful with that vise.
Hints: devise, guise, surprise, exercise, comprise, demise

AFFECT (noun or verb) Actions will affect affection.
All work affects the result eventually.
High tide can affect a ship aground.
Hints: afford, after, afire, afloat, about, ashore, affluent

AGAINST Again, he was against a good cause.
The rain hit against the window.
A gain against is an achievement.
Hints: pain, plain, stain, lain, strain, quaint, paint, contain

AISLE His wife wore paisley down the aisle.
h)   The audience paid extra for aisle seats.
The fair bride walked down the aisle.
Hints: said, maid, laid, fail, sail, dais, raise, rail, hail

A LOT (2 words not 1) I like you a lot.
A lot of good it will do for the lot of us.
It was a small lot next to a large plot.
Hints: a fox, a box, a pot, a mop, a dot, a spot, a toy, a cot

AMONG It was a mongrel among thoroughbreds.
Among the strong men, I select Atlas.
John was among those with long beards.
Hints: song, bong, tong, tongue, Hong Kong, Congo, thong, pongee

AMOUNT What amount should I pay for a mount? (saddle horse)
A mound can be a large amount.
Did the bird moult a large amount?
Hints: mouse, mouth, mountaineer, mourn, amour, mouton

ANALYSIS Paralysis requires analysis.
Dialysis is prescribed after analysis.
Do you have an analysis of Lysol?
Hints: reply, plywood, lily, rarely, rely, wily, daily

ANALYZE Let's analyze the zebra's stripes.
They will analyze as they theorize.
He will analyze rather than apologize.
Hints: recognize, agonize, size, civilize, zeppelin, criticize

ANSWER Were you able to answer the question?
His answer was to swerve the car.
Jack's answer was to swear.
Hints: swim, sweat, swirl, swat, swing, swatch, swig, sweet

APPARENT It is apparent that you were never a parent.
For no apparent reason, he paid the rent.
Was there an apparent need for a parenthesis?
Hints: area, aren't, tenth, rend, glare, spare, stare, pare, trend

APPRECIATE His boss would appreciate precise work.
Does she appreciate her precious possessions?
We hope property values will appreciate not depreciate.
Hints: recite, decimal, decision, special, species, decimate

APPROACH Approach the roach slowly.
The coach explained the new approach.
Do not broach the new approach at this time.
Hints: goat, poach, reproach, encroach, loach, loaf, oaf

APPROXIMATE Apples are approximate in size.
His approach was approximate in style to mine.
Will you approve an approximate quantity?
Hints: inclimate, primate, decimate, appraise, apprehend

ARTHRITIS (Not arthuritis) Arthritis is not spelled like
Arthur with ''itis''.
Ignore thrift when battling arthritis.
Her arthritis seemd to thrive in that climate.
Hints: thrill, thrice, enthrall, thrust, throes, three, forthright

ARTICLE A popsicle was the only frozen article.
Will a pickle tickle his fickle appetite?
The particle was not mentioned in the article.
Hints: disciple, clean, cleave, participle, Pericles, cleat,
leave

ATE The child ate the date on his plate.
h)   The bear's mate ate the honey.
Joseph ate his lunch late.

Hints: gate, sate, fate, abate, rate, grate, hate, collate, later

ATHLETE An athlete prefers a shower to a bath
The first athlete raced down the path.
Do not bother the athlete for an autograph now.
Hints: lath, lathe, mathematics, hath, wrath, thrive, thrust

BARE The hare's cupboard was bare.
h)   The bare baby was cold while in their care.
I do not care to bare all my secrets.
Hints: mare, pare, share, rare, beware, scare, dare, wares

BEAR The circus bear had a tear in his underwear.
h)   A bee lodged in the bear's ear.
Have no fear of my pet bear.
Hints: wear, gear, hear, near, pear, sear, rear, year, clear

BEER This beer tastes queer.
h)   Steer clear of my beer!
Don't peer at your beer; drink it.
Hints: deer, seer, sneer, veer, eerie, cheer, chanticleer, leer

BIER A bier was on the pier.
h)   The second bier is heavier than the first bier.
The crier approached the bier.
Hints: drier, frier, soldier, trier, prettier, gaudier, Currier

BLEW The brewing storm blew a gale.
h)   Alice's son blew out the few candles on his cake.
The crew watched as the wind blew into the sail.
Hints: flew, stew, grew, brew, sew, drew, Andrew, steward

BLUE "True Blue" is a very good title.
h)   Her blue scarf was the clue.
A blue sky presents a pleasant hue.
Hints: cue, due, glue, flue, issue, pursue, suede, duet, sue

BOARD (noun or verb) The board was made into an oar.
h)   That boar could smash a board.
    A scrounger will hoard a good board.
Hints: roar, soar, oarlock, oarsman, hoarse, hoarfrost

BORED An adored matador was gored by a bored bull.
h)   Jane was bored as she pored over her homework.
    The bored cook ignored cored apples.
Hints: before, implore, chore, encore, more, borer, shore, store

BOUILLON Do you like bouillon soup? Oui. ("Yes" in
h)   French)
    Can you play bouillote after you finish your bouillon?
    Oui.
    Was the bouillabaise as tasty as the bouillon? Oui.
Hints: (Try to remember the spelling of the word "yes"
    in French, OUI. It starts like the word "out". Try to
    recall that the middle letter, the U, is pronounced in
    bouillon. The O and I are extra. Or, you might think
    of: Don't throw OUt the bouillon; I want it.)

BRAKE Take a rest; apply your brake.
h)   Don't step on the brake as you near the lake.
    If the brake is not used, a car can make a mess.
Hints: cake, snake, shake, rake, wake, fake, quake, stake, sake

BREAD Take rolls instead of bread.
h)   New cooks dread making bread.
    Knead bread; don't tread on it.
Hints: bead, dead, head, lead, read, plead, cleave, leave, weave

BREAK Do not break the beaker.
h)   A creak usually means a break.
    If you break a seal, it will leak.
Hints: beak, teak, freak, tweak, streak, wreak, peak, sneak, weak

BRED Alfred has bred good dogs.

h)   Fred needed credit to buy the red edition.
   Ted made his bed, fed the dog, and led him to the
   yard.

Hints: wed, Ned, awed, sawed, meddle, predator, redo,
   credit

BULLION The bullion was lifted by pulley.

h)   Some bullion was made into bullets.
   Gold bullion can buy many bulls.

Hints: cull, full, gull, lull, mull, mullet, null, pull

BUSINESS A bus business is usually lucrative.
   A good salesman will hustle up more business.
   His business needs more customers.

Hints: dust, lust, gust, rust, must, bust, crust, disgust

BUSY Buster was busy with his bone.
   Jeff's music has a busy beat.
   Cal was busy with his dusty, rusty car.

Hints: must, just, trust, crust, cuspid, disgust, gust, bust

CANVAS My tent was made of old canvas.

h)   The mast supported a vast canvas.
   Let's use this can as a vase.

Hints: gas, has, task, ask, bask, cask, vascular, masticate

CANVASS Pollsters canvass a mass of people.

h)   The canvass team did not pass this way.
   Please canvass your neighbors for donations for new
   glass.

Hints: bass, crass, grass, lass, jackass, assistant, assorted

CAREFUL Chris was careful not to be wasteful.
   I'll be grateful if he's very careful.
   The faithful were careful when saying their prayers.

Hints: hopeful, woeful, spiteful, delightful, Fulbright,
   hateful

CARELESS If you are careless, you may become car less.

A careless person will prepare less efficiently.

He is rarely careless at home.

Hints: aware, beware, stare, snare, blare, Claire, billionaire

CATEGORY Will the cat eat the gory bird?

Allegory is not the category.

Does it indicate the category?

Hints: allocate, catechism. caterer, dedicate, rate, grate

CEDE Will he cede his decision to recede?

h)   If no one intercedes, he will cede.

When Alfred I cedes, will Alfred II accede to the throne?

Hints: antecede, concede, precede, retrocede, secede

CENT Mary knows that cent is a part of the word century.

h)   They did not create a new cent for the bicentennial.

Recently, I found a new cent.

Hints: decent, docent, scent, accent, descent, central

CENTS Save your cents to pay for recent tax increases.

h)   Any decent candy can no longer be purchased for five cents.

It costs many cents to purchase one scent.

Hints: ascent, descent, docent, accent, centered, central, decent

CERTAIN How can you be certain that it will rain?

Are you certain this pertains to the subject?

I am certain they will detain you unless you explain.

Hints: complain, main, stain, vain, pain, train, retain, gain

CHIEF The chief caught the thief.

Disbelief brought grief to the chief.

Our chief's favorite dessert is pie.

Hints: lie, die, fries, relief, complies, supplies, beautifies

CHOICE Joyce was my choice for a partner.
I will voice my choice.
Some mice ate my nice, choice rice.
Hints: dice, slice, suffice, thrice, price, lice, vice, twice

CHOOSE I can choose too.
Please choose a good melody.
Children choose to call a train a choo choo.
Hints: boost, woo, loose, soot, boot, moon, soon, loon,
boon

CHOSE He chose the small nose, I suppose.
They chose the wrong road.
She chose to pose near the thorny rose bush.
Hints: lose, close, those, whose, cosy, prose, hose,
Joseph, closet

CITE Please cite your opinion when you recite.
h)   Did he cite lucite?
Among other products, he will cite anthracite.
Hints: incite, excite, plebiscite

CLOTHES June loathes buying clothes for others.
The little girl dresses her doll in clothes of cloths.
Margaret disliked her mother's clothes.
Hints: bothers, brothers, pother, betrothes, apothecary,

COMPARATIVE That comparative situation was not
relative.
His dilative solution was not comparative.
Joe's comparative description of a native was creative.
Hints: meditative, derivative, superlative, preparative

CONDEMN Let's not condemn the solemnity of their
religion.
Is it not better to indemnify than to condemn?
A condemner will condemn, not condone.
Hints: concise, concur, demon (delete O), hymnal

CONSCIENCE Anyone who cheats science has no conscience.

Joan's conscience kept her conscious of good and evil.

Lack of a conscience could affect scientific data.

Hints: (Note that IE is used after C against rule).

consume, consent, school, conscientious, convenience, salience, obedience

CONSCIENTIOUS A scientist is a conscientious, ambitious person.

A conscientious butcher will have his scale checked frequently for his clients.

The scientific report had been done by a conscientious team.

Hints: pretentious, contentious, consecutive, conscious. conscript

CONSCIOUS A conscious consensus was needed.

I was conscious of his being serious and gracious.

Was she conscious when she ate the delicious meal?

Hints: luscious, conspicuous, capricious, conscientious, spouse

CONSIDER Must we consider the queen's consort?

Let's consider a sidewalk at the seaside.

Consider those who reside by the wayside.

Hints: insider, beside, sideways, sidesaddle, side, considerable

CONTINUOUS My arduous task was continuous.

His actions were continuous and ambiguous.

A continuous performance can be strenuous.

Hints: contiguous, tenuous, superfluous, sensuous, strenuous

CONVENIENCE The bus was a convenience for her niece.

Owning a genie can be a great convenience.

Having a lenient teacher was a convenience.
Hints: convenient, intervenient, supervenient, advenient

CRITICISM Racism is a form a criticism.
Your criticism of circumcism was rude.
Pacificism can often provoke criticism.
Hints: mysticism, fanaticism, cynicism, lyricism, exorcism

CRITICIZE Do not criticize or fanaticize.
Don will be ostracized if you criticize.
People will criticize if you Anglicize.
Hints: italicize, disorganize, moralize, scepticize, Scotticize

CURIOSITY If curiosity kills a cat, is there no cure?
The guru's mural was a curiosity.
A jury's curiosity is important.
Hints: curt, durable, rural, lure, cursory, hurt, turkey, furious

CURIOUS She was so curious; I was furious.
A curious child can be injurious.
Minnie tried to lure the curious turkey.
Hints: pious, lurid, curt, fury, cursory, insidious, fastidious

CURRICULUM The same curriculum is recurrent year
after year.
A furrier was listed in the curriculum.
Currant and curry making were not part of the curriculum
Hints: purr, hurried, surrey, current, burrow, furrow, flurry

CYMBAL The clang of the cymbal affected the cymba
h) of his ear.
The dancer struck the cymbal with the palm of her
hand.
He found the cymbal near the hymnal.

Hints: cymbidium, decimal, cyma, gimbal, policy maker, homonym

DEALT The past tense for deal is dealt not dealed.
The realtor dealt with wealthy clients.
Life had dealt him wealth but not health.
Hints: meal, heal, peal, stealth, real, zealous, jealous, appeal

DEAR John dear, do you hear me?
h)   Her children were very near and dear to her.
Sue's dear pet clearly did not fear the intruder.
Hints: sear, pear, rear, gear, Lear, tear, ear, appear, bear

DEER Avoid deer crossings when you steer.
h)   The deer acted queer after drinking beer.
Deer at crossings cause cars to veer.
Hints: leer, sheer, seer, jeer, sneer, gazetteer, eerie, cheer

DEPENDENT (or -ANT for someone relying on another for support)
Joseph is dependent on his dentist.
The accident made him dependent on others.
The Occidental's dependent (-ant) was not injured.
Hints: denture, resplendent, indent, dental, indenture, resident

DESERT A desert wasteland appears infertile and
h)   deserted.
Insert a photo of a desert.
A berserk dog may desert its master.
Hints: (Pronounced like a treat but not as pleasant.)
resort, reserve, deserve, conserve, servant, consort, presort, preserve

DESIRABILITY The ability to be desired is desirability.
Desi's desirability eventually waned.
Desirability not suitability was his criteria.
Hints: capability, applicability, destiny, advisability, deserve

DESIRE My desire is to retire.
  Do you desire a new desk?
  I desire to name my horse "De Sire".
Hints: design, desert, desist, destiny, respire, destination

DESPAIR Let's not despair; I found the desk.
  The despot destroyed his kingdom.
  Don't despair; we'll reach the depot in time.
Hints: destruction, desire, bides, desecrate, desist, descreen

DESSERT Tess ate her new dessert messily.
h) Jesse's favorite dessert is ice cream.
  Joe had less dessert than Jim.
Hints: (Sounds similar to the sandy area but tastes good.)
  kiss, assert, gusset, gesso, lesser, gasser, mass, Cressida,
  press

DIFFERENCE Our difference is in pence.
  A stiff penalty sometimes makes no difference.
  When was Biff miffed by the difference?
Hints: stiffer, buffer, conference, skiff, cuff, hence,
  insistence

DIFFERENT A different apartment will differ in rent.
  He was different because he was affluent.
  It was a different staff that took over the plane.
Hints: huffy, stuff, gruff, cuff, insistent, absent, accident, anent

DISAPPOINT The squirrel will disappear if you disappoint
  him.
  This apple may disappoint you.
  The supper did not disappoint her.
Hints: happy, snappy, approve, appoint, grapple, napper,
  Trapp

DISASTROUS Joel's disastrous past haunted him.
  The lustrous beam proved most disastrous.
  The stray bullet was disastrous.
Hints: strike, straight, strafe, astral, strain, strode, strap

DISCIPLINE Disco surely lacks discipline.
Discipline was not needed by the disciples.
A disciform has discipline.
Hints: disclaim, discuss, discus, disciplinary, discifloral

DISEASE We hope to make disease disappear.
Having a disease would displease me.
That disease is visible when you disrobe.
Hints: discus, dismiss, display, dispute, disdain, disrupt, disk

DIVINE Divide your divine cake now.
Dior creates divine gowns for divas.
She discovered a divine diet.
Hints: dive, divot, divulge, dip, diorama, digest, disk, discern

EFFECT (noun, sometimes a verb)
The result was the effect of efficient work.
Its effect was obvious to Jeff, the referee.
The teflon pan gave the desired effect.
Hints: clef, hefty, lefty, weft, before, befriend, refer, defer

EFFICIENT A deficient product is not efficient.
The wrong coefficient was not efficient.
Efficient work is better than deficient work.
Hints: expedient, salient, client, scientific, calorifient

EIGHT The pregnant cat carried a lot of weight—
h)   eight fetuses.
My sleigh can carry eight plus freight.
His paperweight weighs eight ounces.
Hints: height, sleight, eighty, underweight, heavyweight

EMBARRASS Do not embarrass the girl with a barrage
of crass remarks.
Purchasing a barrel of wine would embarrass him.
To quarrel with the lass in public would embarrass me.
Hints: carrot, asset, arrive, arrange, quarry, brass, assist

EQUIPMENT Strip the equipment!
Don't quip about his choice of equipment.
This equipage contains my equipment.
Hints: sip, dip, grip, flip, zip, stripe, ripe, trip, slip, snip

EQUIPPED Len's lab was equipped then stripped.
After being equipped, fear of the cost gripped him.
The newly-equipped lab was ripped apart by a tornado.
Hints: quipped, tripped, dipped, skipped, flipped, slipped

ESPECIALLY The airport was not especially busy because of the rally.
That species is not especially important to the tally.
His Vespa was especially small.
Hints: respect, espouse, vesper, whisper, ally, Sally, dally

EXAGGERATE A nagger might tend to exaggerate.
Do not exaggerate your ragged costume.
Anne likes to exaggerate her goggles' value.
Hints: stagger, lugger, hugger, defogger, bagger, tagger, tugger

EXCELLENCE Studying in silence leads to excellence in grades.
Excellence at work could lead to loads of pence.
Excellence can be a convenience.
Hints: whence, fence, commence, hence, diligence, incidence

EXCELLENT Sharon does have an excellent cello.
This repellent is excellent.
You have an excellent cellular phone.
Hints: ballet, ballot, paella, cellar, embellish, cell, cellist

EXCITABLE The fable he told was excitable.
The parable had an excitable ending.
Clark Gable's movies were excitable.
Hints: cable, Mabel, sable, table, stable, durable, liable

EXERCISE Precise exercise is important but do not
overexert.
Rex had to devise exercise for his pet ibex.
The next exercise is easier.
Hints: lexicon, dexterous, excise, concise, texture, hex,
text, next

EXPENSE An expanse of land is an expense.
Let's dispense with the extra expense.
They will recompense for the tinsel expense.
Hints: condense, sense, rinse, tense, pensive, compensate,
dense

EXPERIENCE Practice makes perfect, hence experience.
It was an eerie science experience.
From my experience trying to scale it, I knew the fence
was too high.
Hints: conscience, pence, whence, penitence, incidence,
pestilence.

EXPERIMENT Did you verify the experiment?
The spherical experiment lasted all period.
An expert will experiment to achieve experience.
Hints: derision, verily, meridian, derive, Pericles, veritable

EXPLANATION His explanation of the plan was clear.
Plano had no explanation for the plankton on the plane.
There was no explanation for the swollen gland.
Hints: lanolin, land, splash, plant, planet, plank, place,
play

EXTREMELY The remedy is extremely painful.
Timely caution is extremely helpful.
That creme was extremely thick.
Hints: frame, tame, game, same, comely, lame, timely, ·
namely

FAIR Allen's offer to repair the stair was fair.
h) Was the girl with blonde hair fair?

To compare us with Fred and Adele Astaire is not fair.
Hints: lair, air, chair, pair, debonair, Airedale, airplane

FARE (1) Tom paid the fare on a dare.
h)   Shall we share the fare?
Would a hare pay the fare?
Hints: care, bare, flare, mare, scare, beware, pare, snare,
rare (see FARE 2 below)

FARE (2) My niece will fare well with good nursing
h)   care.
Did you fare well on the old mare?
He would not fare well in a bare room.
Hints: scare, flare, ware, rare, stare, pare, hare, beware

FASCINATE Fascists do not fascinate people.
Fast food fascinates children.
Loofas (sponges) fascinate first-time buyers.
Hints: last, gash, hash, mash, past, task, was, wasp, mast

FAVORITE My favorite "bite" is chocolate.
Oscar's favorite kite is very colorful.
A favorite food can incite an appetite.
Hints: reunite, sprite, iterate, cite, white, rite, site, spite

FAZE Larry's gaze did not faze her.
h)   An order to raze the building would faze the tenants.
The blaze did not faze the grazing cattle.
Hints: craze, daze, haze, laze, gaze, amaze, braze, azalea

FEAT The sword swallower's feat involved using heat.
h)   A circus performer's feat earns him money to eat.
Providing meat and wheat was a neat feat.
Hints: beat, treat, peat, seat, threat, cheat, leather,
weather

FEET Paul's feet were red as a beet.
h)   His queer feet stuck out of the sheet.
Biff's feet were the largest in the fleet.

Hints: sweet, screen, preen, queen, fleece, wee, week, meek

FICTITIOUS A repetitious plot may seem fictitious.
Good fictitious stories are ambitious undertakings.
His fictitious plot dealt with superstitious beliefs.
Hints: expeditious, propitious, seditious, factitious

FIELD A field of daisies may yield a bouquet.
Shield that field from the sprayer.
Our yield from the upper field was small.
Hints: wield, wiener, pie, lie, die, Audie, Susie

FLEW A new robin flew out of the nest.
h)   When the wind blew, the leaves flew.
The dew flew off the trees when the wind blew.
Hints: drew, grew, crew, few, chew, withdrew, sew, hew, yew

FLUE The chimney flue cleaning was due.
h)   A dirty flue can spoil a blue sky.
Glue cannot repair a cracked flue.
Hints: clue, cue, ensue, hue, rue, accrue, fuel, duel, cruel

FOR Is this letter for me or for you?
h)   Let's mount High Tor for the view.
A strong cord did the work for me.
Hints: port, sort, ford, parlor, word, torn, torte, worn, scorn

FORE "Fore!" shouted the golfer before playing
h)   through.
A foreman of a jury is chosen before the other members.
The weather man can usually forecast storms before they occur.
Hints: bore, core, more, sore, tore, wore, Azores, pore, lore

FOREIGN A king may reign in a foreign country.
  The queen's peignoir was of foreign origin.
  Do not deign to speak a word foreign to you.
Hints: feign, interreign, misfeign, seigneur

FORTH Let's go forth for a stroll.
h) Is it worthwhile going forth to the fort?
  The worthless ship went forth from the port.
Hints: sort, worthy, forthright, forte, forty, sport, short,
  horse

FORTY The class is scheduled for forty minutes.
  Shorty just turned forty.
  It's forty miles to the fort.
Hints: worth, torte, sort, port, bore, core, Mortimer, lore,
  pore

FORWARD Let's go forward not rearward.
  The forward passes sent the ball toward the doorway.
  Irwin continued forward.
Hints: otherwise, overwise, cornerwise, counterweight

FOUR Chester can devour four pizzas at one sitting.
h) Those four lemons are all sour.
  Four men went on a tour.
Hints: flour, scour, pour, our, your, course, dour, gourmet

FOURTH It was the fourth day of the trial in room four.
h) Can he devour a fourth portion?
  I've scoured this pot for the fourth and last time.
Hints: flour, sour, your, course, dour, pour, gourmet,
  hour, amour

FRIEND Would a good friend lie to you?
  A friend is not a fiend.
  My friend enjoyed the bicentenial pies.
Hints: cries, pries, grieve, hie, Aries, brie, tried, reprieve

FULFILL Alfred took the Gulf tour to fulfill his new job
  requirement.

After the first lone L, there are two L's in fulfill.
Be careful not to overfill the glasses when you fulfill
your duties.

Hints: spiteful, soulful, self, regretful, hateful, cupful, elf

Note: This word may also be spelled fulfil but fulfill is
most common.

FUNDAMENTAL Do you think he will fund a mental
health plan?
The fundamental lesson was a mental stimulant.
Their fundamental plan will be lamentable if carried
through.

Hints: inundate, amen, dame, dam, Damon, laminate,
lame, tame

GNU The gnu at the zoo is a nuisance.
h)   The new gnu was numb.
Don't nudge the gnu!

Hints: nun, nuance, nub, nut, null, nullify, nuclear, nurse

GRAMMAR Grandma knew her grammar.
Do not mar my grammar book.
They used poor grammar in the drama.

Hints: mark, Mars, marsh, Mary, Omar, mama, Marion,
marshal

GRATE Don't catch your heel in the grate. What a fate!
h)   Grate the cheese at a slow rate.
You'll grate the gate! Too late.

Hints: crate, irate, create, orate, date, equate, mate, sate

GREAT The turkey and stuffing were a great treat.
h)   Cherries are great to eat.
Did you see that great Preakness race?

Hints: dream, cream, beam, read, heat, meat, peat, seat,
break

GUARANTEE One can guard against losses with a guarantee.

Guard my auntie. (antee)
Gubernatorial candidates cannot guarantee their promises.
Hints: gullible, language, guava, guide, guru, Ragu, Gucci, Jaguar

GUIDANCE Guidance when learning to dance is helpful.
Guidance will enhance your craft.
Guidance is required for the proper stance in fencing.
Hints: prance, glance, entrance, pants, fancy, lance, trance

GUIDING The guide lost his E while guiding.
Your helpful guiding prevented us from sliding.
Guiding is easy when riding a horse.
Hints: siding, wading, hiding, tidings, biding, confiding, did

HAY "Hay is for horses", they say.
h)   This bale of hay may last all day.
Is that the way to pitch hay?
Hints: ray, stray, quay, bay, Fay, Kay, may, tray, strap, wrap

HEAR Can you hear with your right ear?
h)   The deaf may appear to hear.
Did you hear the bear, dear?
Hints: rear, year, fear, tear, gear, near, pear, spear, sear

HEIGHT The height of the plant was eight inches.
He had the height and build of a welterweight.
She is underweight for her height.
Hints: (EI not after a C, against rule.) eighty, sleigh, paperweight, heavyweight
Note: There is no third H in height (heighth).

HERE Here comes the parade. Where? Over there.
h)   It's a mere 50 feet from here.
Were you here earlier?

Hints: rev_ere, sev_ere, aust_ere, her_eby, s_ere, coh_erent, her_edity

HEY H_ey you! Where are th_ey going?
h)   H_ey! Who took Miss Muffet's wh_ey?
    H_ey! You can't surv_ey lakes in Monter_ey.
Hints: conv_ey, donk_ey, disob_ey, k_ey, dov_ey, ospr_ey, pr_ey, gr_ey

HOLE Let's punch a h_ole with a p_ole.
h)   The m_ole ducked into a h_ole.
    There's a h_ole in my t_ole tray.
Hints: _oleo, d_ole, s_ole, T_oledo, st_ole, r_ole, _oleander, con-d_olence

HORS D'OEUVRES Jan ab_hors h_ors d'_oeuvres.
    The h_ors(e) and d_oe come first in h_ors d'_oeuvres.
    Hors d'_oeuvres require some maneuvers.
Hints: mane_uvers (_vres), lo_uvers (_vres)

HOUR Can we really measure an h_our with an h_ourglass?
h)   Is this y_our h_our for tennis?
    The large hand on _our clock denotes the h_our.
Hints: f_our, p_our, s_our, d_our, dev_our, vel_our, am_our, t_our

HUGE The place of refu_ge was hu_ge.
    Scroo_ge made a hu_ge adjustment.
    Her rou_ge appeared as 2 hu_ge spots on her cheeks.
Hints: stoo_ge, subterfu_ge, lu_ge, gau_ge, ra_ge, pa_ge, sta_ge, enga_ge

HUNGRY The hun_gry lion was an_gry.
    _Greg's mon_grel is hun_gry.
    A hun_gry o_gre ate an e_gret.
Hints: _greet, _great, de_grease, di_gress, de_grade, hung, lung

IGNORANCE Ign_orance ran in the family.
    One c_annot m_anage a r_anch with ign_orance.
    They missed their ch_ance because of ignor_ance.

Hints: trance, prance, enhance, stance, glance, romance, dance

I'LL (I WILL) I'll (I will) do it when I get home.
h)   I'll (I will) diet very soon.
Let's watch the time or I'll (I will) be late.
Hints: (See words in parenthesis.)

INDISPENSABLE In "dis" pen, sable is king.
Clark Gable's appendicitis was not indispensable.
A good discus is indispensable to a capable thrower.
Hints: fable, table, lisp, crisp, sister, cable, risen, dispute

INFLUENTIAL To be influential, power is not essential.
The river current was influential in flooding the valley.
An influential person may be fluent when discussions are needed.
Hints: justice, martial, entire, entice, potential, apprentice

INTEREST I have no interest in becoming an intern.
Ryan's avid interest in the intercom improved his work.
In the interim, his interest waned.
Hints: winter, interval, hinder, interact, intersect, binder

INTERFERE Do not interfere here.
No one will interfere while we revere.
A severe fire would interfere with wildlife growth.
Hints: before, fare, fore, mere, austere, sere, were, reread

INTERPRET Didn't he pretend to interpret Terry's note?
Can you interpret the pretty egret's language?
Let me try to interpret the words for the printer.
Hints: winter, Pinter, regret, pretentious, interpose, fret

INTERPRETATION Interpretation requires preparation.
His interpretation was just a pretense.
Our own interpretation of the Preamble differs.
Hints: present, prepare, press, precise, presuppose, precocious

INTERRUPT It is dangerous to interrupt a terrorist.
The internal rupture may not interrupt the flow of oil.
If you interrupt, I will make an error.
Hints: terra, terrible, terrain, terrapin, corrupt, correct

IRRELEVANT The location of the elevator was
irrelevant.
Levitation is irrelevant in this case.
A fever level can never be irrelevant.
Hints: lever, leverage, clever, Levine, Leviticus, levee,
levant

ISLE Do they have any lisle on the isle?
h)   An islet is a small isle.
Mislead contains the word isle.
Hints: aisle, island, grisly, gristmill, pristine, Islam

IT'S It's (It is) his book.
h)   It's (It is) six o'clock.
Tell me when it's (it is) time to go home.
Hints: (The apostrophe signifies that a letter is missing.
When "it is" cannot be substituted, use "its".)

ITS That animal lives by its wits.
h)   My pet likes its scrap bits.
A dog usually sits by its master.
Hints: hits, pits, fits, flits, grits, quits, writs, knits, skits

KNEW Alma knew that I had a new dress.
h)   Drew knew that they would hew the yew.
The crew knew him by name.
Hints: dew, few, threw, stew, sew, knife, knave, knee,
knead

KNOW Does the knight know how to joust?
h)   Did you know that I hurt my knee?
Did you know that a cow could mow your lawn?
Hints: wow, owl, throw, escrow, row, knit, knot, knife,
knave

KNOWLEDGE The badger showed no knowledge of the owl.
Do you know how to trim the hedge?
I know where the edge is.
Hints: fidget, midget, ridge, bowled, howled, knee, knot, knit

LABOR We labor for money.
Boring labor lacks flavor.
The parlor organ required some labor.
Hints: more, work, score, chore, aorta, border, sort, Porgy, pore

LABORATORY A scientist will labor in his laboratory.
Oratory is not heard in a science laboratory.
Laboratory work may be gory.
Hints: word, score, more, lore, border, cord, fort, short, port

LABORER A borer is a laborer.
A kitchen laborer uses a corer.
That laborer will get a sore back.
Hints: pore, wore, adore, store, tore, before, shore, yore, gore

LAID With aid, he laid the cornerstone.
Jane paid to have the bricks laid.
The lioness laid down her cub in the lair.
Hints: pail, mail, hair, said, maid, wail, sail, tail, retail

LATER The food hater ate later.
You may skate later, when the water is frozen.
I will sate my appetite later.
Hints: dater, cater, fate, gate, eater, atelier, mate, state, rate

LEAD (1) Lead the thread into the bead.
h)   The teacher will lead the reading.
The student at the head of the line will lead.

Hints: each, teach, advise, adept, leach, preach, reach, peach, dead (See LEAD 2 below.)

LEAD (2) Do not tread on the lead pipe.
h) Let's spread the lead paint.
We'll use lead instead.
Hints: dread, bread, read, great, steadfast, dead, tread, head

LED The nurse led the child to bed.
h) James led the line with his sled.
Ted fled; the medic bled.
Hints: fed, Ned, pedal, sped, wed, chafed, pined, saddled

LEISURE Hawaiian leis invite you to enjoy your leisure.
Enjoy leisure by the Seine.
Seize your leisure when you can.
Hints: heist, Seiko, heiress, height, neigh, sleigh, heifer
(If letters have an A sound, EI is correct.)

LENGTH Clang the bell at length.
Peggy can speak at length in any language.
The silent G in length makes spelling difficult.
Hints: harangue, languish, dengue, merengue, hang, bingo, sing

LENGTHENING We are lengthening the language class period.
"Then" is in the word lengthening.
Leng then began lengthening the noodles.
Hints: merengue, tongue, languish, them, they, English, angle

LIAISON The A is between two I's in liaison.
Let's arrange a liaison at the Maison Rouge.
Ian acted as liaison between 2 hospital aides.
Hints: aisle, liable, Iago, pliable, reliable, liar, familiar

LICENSE Fifty cents will not buy a license.

Use of incense requires no license.
No license? Police will ticket you.
Hints: slice, mice, ice, spice, rice, licentious, nice, center

LIKENESS Ike's old likeness hung over the mike.
My bike's likeness to his was amazing.
The tyke's likeness to his new father was startling.
Hints: dike, hike, strike, pike, like, spike, shrike, Riker, piker

LOGISTICS Let's not clog the logistics with extra details.
Poor logistics in the fog failed the rogue.
Bogus logistics can often be dangerous.
Hints: dog, gist, agog, hog, log, cog, gesso, drag, stag, rag, bag

LOOSE The loose goose chased the moose.
The caboose is loose.
The noose was too loose.
Hints: boo, zoo, moo, moon, woo, boom, room, zoom, wood, Roo, took.

LOOSER Make the scarf looser or you will be too warm.
The looser tool was a boon to the project.
Stack the wood looser so it can dry out.
Hints: good, mood, zoom, stool, spool, pool, fool, cool, drool

LOSE Did you lose the rose?
You will lose your pet if you do not close the gate.
I might lose my hose if I expose it to the elements.
Hints: chose, nose, repose, pose, dispose, suppose, compose

LOSER He chose a loser when he hired Jake.
Lois will be the loser if she gets closer to the patient.
A good poser will never be a loser in modelling.

Hints: repo_ser, expo_ser, do_ser, clo_set, explo_sive, fro_st, pro_se

(<u>A</u>) <u>LOT</u> (Listed under A)

LUXURY The ju_ry had the lux_ury of eating in a restaurant.
Her show of lux_ury created a fu_ry in her neighbors.
June wants to bu_ry herself in lux_ury.
Hints: pu_re, ru_ral, su_re, lu_rid, cu_r, du_rable, cu_rable, bu_y

MADE Susie finally ma_de the gra_de.
h) Da_de ma_de an adequa_te sha_de.
Nancy ma_de the bed and then relaxed with some lemonade.
Hints: ba_de, fa_de, ja_de, ade_pt, gla_de, spa_de, deca_de, pa-rade

MAID The hotel ma_id la_id the towels on the bed.
h) Their new ma_id wears her ha_ir in a bra_id.
His ma_id is not well pa_id.
Hints: sa_id, sta_id, ra_id, upbra_id, afra_id, unla_id, prepa_id

MAIL Place unwanted ma_il in the pa_il.
h) Ha_il the mail-truck driver.
The ja_iler had ma_il for the sa_ilor at the ja_il.
Hints: sa_il, ra_il, fa_il, ta_il, Ga_il, na_il, a_ileron, ta_ilor, ba_il

MAINTENANCE Tenants pay for main_tenance.
Ten more tenants require extra main_tenance.
Even a ten_t needs maintenance.
Hints: ten_acity, ten_d, ute_nsil, ofte_n, ten_dency, superinte_n-dent

MALE Was the tiger a ma_le or a fema_le?
h) Is the ma_le dog for sa_le?
James became a pa_le ma_le in that ga_le.
Hints: da_le, ba_le, ka_le, ta_le, Ya_le, a_le, wha_le, sha_le, ha_le

MANEUVER Perform the maneu_ver away from the neu_tral zone.

Creation of a neuter form was quite a maneuver.
The European division's quick maneuvering was brilliant.
Hints: neuralgia, neurotic, euro, euphonic, eucalyptus, eugenic

MARRIAGE The marriage will be performed in a carriage.
It was a harried marriage.
They did not quarrel before the marriage.
Hints: curry, marred, parried, carried, tarry, hurry, scurry

MATHEMATICS Ma, the matics are here.
Schematics may contain some mathematics.
The word mathematics contains the word thematics.
Hints: mother, them, acrobatics, aerobics, politics, heretics

MEANT The mean man meant to do harm.
She meant to wean her pet sooner.
His dean meant to encourage Jim's zeal.
Hints: lean, bean, jean, leant, clean, oleander, Orleans, fear

MEAT Let's eat the tender meat.
h)   Heat the meat in the oven.
Each had eaten his fill of the meat.
Hints: peat, seat, neat, beat, great, feat, bleat, leather

MECHANICS The mechanics left nothing to chance for me.
Mechanics help me avoid many panics.
Have the mechanics recharge the system.
Hints: mechanism, Lech, medal, channel, chain, change, hand

MEDICINE The army medic had the medicine.
A medical group has medicine on hand.
Dictate your editorial about medicine today.

Hints: edict, dictum, edifice, edition, dictionary, dice, media

MEET Shall we meet on the street?
h)   When people meet, they greet each other.
  I will meet a sweet girl at the store.
Hints: beet, fleet, sleet, tee, teeter, tweet, sleek, leek

METE Pete will mete out the meat portions.
h)   Lawyers will mete out a complete estate.
  Before the fete, they will mete out the supplies.
Hints: meter, deter, concrete, deplete, excrete, meteor, replete

MINIATURE A miniature may have stature.
  His miniature caricature is clever.
  Mother Nature provides some miniature flowers in Spring.
Hints: mature, sat, pat, hat, Fiat, armature, literature

MISCHIEF The thief started the mischief.
  Mischief might be relieved with a pie.
  The police chief brought some relief from the mischief.
Hints: tie, belief, brie, diet, Juliet, lien, belie, brief

NARRATIVE The narrative was about Barranquilla.
  This narrative will embarrass her.
  Jo's narrative didn't describe the barracuda.
Hints: narrate, warrant, currant, errant, tarragon, parrakeet

NECESSARY An accessory may be necessary.
  Recess is necessary for young children.
  This process is necessary for success.
Hints: excess, cesspool, cess, cessation, business, cesspit

NEW I will have to review the new lesson.
h)   We have a new preview for the interview.
  A gale blew the new tent over.

Hints: dew, pew, few, sew, grew, strew, brew, crew, Drew, hew

NINETY Nine times ten equals ninety.

Ninety contains the word nine.

We met a quartet of ninety-year-olds.

Hints: beget, cadet, inset, let, spinet, cabinet, net, regret

NO No one may enter here now.

h) No, I will not go to play Keno.

Don't go that way; there is no other entrance.

Hints: nor, nod, nothing, not, Norse, none, nog, note, noble

NOTICEABLE We were able to notice a noticeable difference.

A peaceable person usually is not noticeable.

Her laceable undergarment was noticeable.

Hints: panacea, traceable, Rhea, paceable, Medea, Crimea, idea

NOTICING Mary was noticing the icing on the cake.

Noticing an enticing treat is natural.

Everyone was noticing the blue, racing water.

Hints: spicing, dicing, lacing, gracing, tracing, spacing, facing

OBSTACLE The extra staple created an obstacle.

Our star tackle downed his lone obstacle.

A stack of boxes near the door was an obstacle.

Hints: abstain, attaché, staff, stay, stall, stave, photostat

OCCUR When will the fur sale occur?

Did it ever occur to you to feed the cur?

I hope my turn will occur again in this inning.

Hints: durable, hurt, curable, surly, endurable, curt, tour

Note: Occur has only 1 R; all other forms of this word that begin with "occur" have 2 R's.

OCCURRED The ocean current's drop occurred suddenly.

The accident occurred when Murray hurried.

Everyone scurried when the tornado occurred.

Hints: burred, currant, furred, demurred, stirred, referred

OCCURRENCE The graph showed a rare occurrence in currency variations.

The unusual occurrence struck in a hurry.

The current occurrence was short-lived.

Hints: deburred, garrulous, burr, burrow, curry, currier, tarry

OCCURRING Deburring was occurring as he filed.

It won't be occurring or recurring again.

Both events were occurring concurrently.

Hints: parrot, parry, curry, burr, tarry, carry, marry, Larry, scurry

OMIT Did you omit the comet from the drawing?

Mom, did you omit the permit?

Tom will not omit his full signature again.

Hints: emit, foment, gamut, myth, admit, smitten, remit, submit

ONE One alone can be lonely.

h)   One apple a day keeps a body in tone.

One lone cone was left per road zone.

Hints: bone, gone, pone, hone, stone, tone, done, money, monel

OPERATE I hope the new man can operate the machinery.

The backstage crew will not operate the opera curtain.

For a firm to operate properly, employees must cooperate.

Hints: pop, top, sop, cope, lop, roper, slope, antelope, grope

OPPONENT An opponent has an opposite view.

Poppo, the clown, has two P's like opponent.
Each opponent will oppose one person.
Hints: Muppet, guppy, suppose, puppy, scrappy, snappy, topple

OPPOSE Let us suppose that you oppose me.
Mr. Capp does not oppose good rapport.
Some metals, like copper, may oppose others.
Hints: stopper, dropper, guppy, dapper, topper, hopper, gripper

OPTIMISM Tim's optimism was refreshing.
The optician expressed optimism.
Adopting optimism can be beneficial.
Hints: optimum, timing, timber, time, timid, timbal, timetable

ORIGIN In an origin, we have a beginning.
Do you know the origin of gin?
The gist of the story was the origin of the argument.
Hints: ginger, rigid, aging, girl, gingham, ginkgo, gink

ORIGINAL Original is not final.
The original package of ginger was fresher.
Begin with the original script.
Hints: giblet, gin, girl, gist, Ginza, linger, gingham, ginkgo

OUR Let's plan our own tour.
h)   Is that our car or your car?
This is our fourth prize.
Hints: sour, four, pour, dour, amour, mourn, courage, entourage

PAIL Place the pail on the rail.
h)   Hang the pail on the nail.
A pail with a hole will fail when you bail.
Hints: sail, tail, wail, mail, jail, hail, trail, quail, frail

PAIR That is a fair pair of gloves.
h)   The pair of bears slept in their lair.
   This aircraft has a pair of engines.
Hints: air, hair, stair, chair, eclair, flair, mohair, despair

PALE This is a pale ale.
h)   He was very pale for a male.
   The pale whale was for sale at Yale.
Hints: bale, dale, shale, kale, Airedale, scale, gale, tale

PARALLEL Parallel contains the word all.
   All the lines Ellie drew were parallel.
   The valley ran parallel to the mountains.
Hints: ball, call, stall, wall, rally, enthralled, hall, tall

PARE We must pare the cost or share it.
h)   Please pare the fruit with care.
   Don't dare to pare her banana.
Hints: bare, hare, wares, tare, fare, mare, stare, area,
   spare

PASSED Jan passed the course with two S's.
h)   The massed group passed by peacefully.
   Kay passed by her old classroom.
Hints: stressed, pressed, gassed, grassed, glassed, embar-
   rassed

PAST The past is gone; it does not last.
h)   The sail billowed past the mast.
   That astronaut went past the astronomer's view.
Hints: asterisk, plastic, fast, cast, pasture, drastic, master

PEACE A pea in a pod is at peace until the pod is
h)   opened.
   It may appear to be peace.
   To keep peace, they will impeach him.
Hints: pear, rear, cease, decrease, grease, appease,
   tease

PEAR This pear is very dear.
h)   A bear would love this pear.
   This tastes like last year's pear.
Hints: fear, gear, near, sear, earn, early, clear, shear, ear

PERCEIVE I perceive that he will deceive her.
   Do you perceive that you will receive a good grade?
   Can you conceive that he will perceive the truth?
Hints: Seine, leisure, weird, ceiling, misconceive, receipt

PERMANENT The Burma Shave signs were not permanent.
   A man's life is not permanent.
   Armament is not meant to be permanent.
Hints: firmament, mane, humane, manikin, manifold, Roman, manage

PERSISTENT June will usually be persistent to some extent.
   Dad was very persistent when putting up the tent.
   An octopus can be persistent with one tentacle.
Hints: intent, content, pretend, tenacious, insistent, consistent

PERSONAL (See PERSONNEL) Al's personal property is of value to him.
   Personal letters are always private.
   The conversation was already too personal.
Hints: ally, algae, alter, halt, falter, alfalfa, pal, aluminum

PERSONNEL (See PERSONAL) Nellie became an excellent personnel manager.
   A person applies for a new job in a personnel department.
   Personnel files contain N, E, and L folders.
Hints: tunnel, funnel, gunnel, panel, channel, Chanel, crenel

PERSUADE A person can persuade a friend to help.
   Perhaps I can persuade him.

Will you persuade your superior to come for supper?

Hints: persue, peruse, super, perch, pert, period, upper, roper

PERTAIN Certain rules pertain to specific games.

"Pert" will usually pertain to a young person.

"Copper" could pertain to a penny.

Hints: percent, peril, personal, stopper, Gert, keeper, mere, per

PHASE The child's phone phase had ended.

h) One phase of learning to read involves phonetics.

Plot the various phases on a graph.

Hints: phoney, Ralph, physical, photograph, philosophy, phlox

PHILOSOPHY My philosophy involves prompt payment of my sophomore's bills.

The use of philo for strudel is my philosophy.

Philip's philosophy won him a trophy.

Hints: silos, Hilo, Sophie, tile, Gilda, hill, lose, philology

PHYSICAL Physical atrophy can be avoided.

This trophy proves his great physical ability.

My physician gave me a partial physical exam.

Hints: physiology, telegraphy, geography, physicist, physics

PIECE May I have a piece of pie?

h) Does your niece want a piece of candy?

Jane found a piece of shell in her sieve.

Hints: diet, Tootsie, lie, vie, Trieste, tries, pries, skies

PLAYWRIGHT A playwright must play with the right emotions.

The bright playwright has been losing his sight.

Their fight, as described by the playwright, was terrific.

Hints: light, night, might, height, tight, eight, sleight

POINSETTIA Poi comes from the taro root not a poinsettia.

The word point is not in poinsettia.

Please do not spoil my white poinsettia by overwatering it.

Hints: coin, purloin, sirloin, tenderloin, adjoin, loin, joint

PORE Has the pore enlarged more?

h)   June adores to pore over new travel folders.

Let's pore over the best Azores photos.

Hints: core, bore, store, sore, wore, Oregon, ore, implore, tore

POUR Please pour our wine.

h)   Pour out the sour milk.

We must pour our cold drinks ourselves.

Hints: dour, hour, four, detour, velour, flour, courage, entourage

PRECEDE Did Adam precede Eve to Eden?

Let us precede the group before the tide recedes.

Shall we precede them to pick edelweiss?

Hints: concede, federal, edema, redemption, cede, accede, secede

PREFER I prefer the first offer.

The accountant will defer payment if you prefer.

I prefer this type of fern.

Hints: ferment, heifer, confer, reference, conifer, offer, Bert

PREFERRED Jerry preferred the ferry.

The accountant preferred a deferred payment.

Alma preferred to remove the error.

Hints: jarred, barred, erred, conferred, berry, carry, tarry

PREJUDICE Prejudgment is a form of prejudice.

Judith's prejudice affected her judgment.

A judge must show no prejudice.

Hints: juice, jug, judo, juggle, judicious, jugular, juggernaut

PRICING Pricing the icing was difficult.
Pricing of racing tickets varies.
When sacrificing, pricing is important.
Hints: slicing, pacing, spicing, dicing, splicing, tracing

PRIMITIVE A primitive viewpoint can be limiting.
The itinerary led us through a primitive area.
Definitive rhymes with primitive.
Hints: writing, biting, whitish, appendicitis, itinerant, mitigate

PRINCIPAL He was the principal for all the students.
h)   The principal residents in a palace are royalty.
The principal entrée was very palatable.
Hints: palate, palatial, pale, pal, Opal, palette, palm

PRINCIPLE The officers enforced the principle for a couple of months.
It was a principle created by the people.
The principle became a pledge.
Hints: apple, plea, pleasant, pleat, plenary, plead, duplex

PRIVILEGE You are depriving him of his privilege.
Living in the old villa is a privilege.
The villain lost his privileges when he committed the crime.
Hints: vile, vilify, privily, village, civil, civic, victory

PROCEDURE A new process changed the procedure.
This procedure will not be continued when the oil recedes.
The prisoners must cede to the new procedure.
Hints: ceiling, celery, price, celestial, cell, cellar, excel

PROCEED Proceed to plant the seed.
After such a deed, he will proceed to jail.

Don't proceed to feed the fish today.
Hints: freed, heed, knee, peel, reel, reed, creed, need, deem

PROMINENT A prominent denture is uncomfortable.
An eminent person will not be prominent necessarily.
The delinquent became much too prominent in his town.
Hints: sent, went, tent, rent, lent, dent, cent, bent, salient

PSYCHOLOGY Psychology was his first choice.
His choral leader often used psychology on the choir.
"Pyscho" could be a study in psychology.
Hints: chosen, chop, chock, cholera, chow, scholar, choke

PURSUE The purser will pursue the stowaway.
Pursue the purple purse snatcher.
A puritan would pursue his religious purpose.
Hints: pure, purge, purl, puree, purchase, purify, purloin, purely

QUANTITY A quantum is a stated quantity.
The scant quantity caused him to rant.
I want a large quantity of scrap.
Hints: entity, title, antidote, anticlimax, canter, pant, rant

RAIN We gain from the rain.
h)   It's starting to rain on the train again.
Too much rain may not drain.
Hints: grain, strain, brain, refrain, sprain, Spain, main

READ (1) The leader will read first.
h)   What I read stays in my head.
I did read the bread recipe incorrectly.
Hints: bead, plead, knead, each, mislead, reach, peach, teach
Note: Today I read; yesterday I read; tomorrow I will read. (see READ 2 below).

READ (2) Sue ate her bread while I read.
h)   Have you read the Dead Sea Scrolls?
He read instead of using the treadmill.
Hints: misread, dread, thread, mislead, tread, spread, ahead

REAL It was a real diamond, a good deal.
h)   Did she conceal the real veal?
Would a real seal heal that quickly?
Hints: peal, teal, zeal, congeal, reveal, meal, repeal, appeal

RECEIVE I perceive he will not receive a birthday card.
Did your cousin receive a postcard of the Seine?
My vein is too small for me to receive an injection.
Hints: conceive, deceive, receipt, ceiling, ceiba

RECEIVING Will she be receiving the peignoir today?
Receiving edelweiss is a great pleasure.
His receiving contraband was deceiving.
Hints: ceiling, heifer, Seine, reign, vein, stein, rein

RED We fed the red bird.
h)   The red drink led to his early demise.
Carrie's bed had a red and blue bedspread.
Hints: tired, hired, lured, Keds, sired, mired, reduce, cured

REED Indeed, the oboe is a reed instrument.
h)   Heed the reed sound.
There is a need for another reed player.
Hints: breed, seed, deed, greed, feed, teed, steed, creed, veer

REEL He liked the feel of a new fishing reel.
h)   Troy's reel brought him a small eel.
An eelworm on the reel looked eerie.
Hints: peel, heel, keel, creel, teenager, queer, creep, spleen

REFERRING Were you referring to the herring?
The teacher was referring to the error.
The boss knew that the errand you were referring to
had been done.
Hints: concurring, deferring, conferring, deterring, erring

REIGN It happened during the reign of the sovereign,
h)   King Henry VIII.
This was the queen's peignoir during her reign.
An imposter might feign noble birth and reign.
Hints: foreign, seignior, deign, interreign, reignite,

RELATIVE Relatives are related to one another by birth.
The native was someone's relative.
I have a very talkative relative.
Hints: superlative, relativity, latent, relation, latrine, lath

RELIEVE Mamie won't relieve her sieve.
I will relieve you of that piece of pie.
Don't lie to me even if it will relieve your fear of re-
ceiving punishment.
Hints: flies, brie, tie, specie, retrieve, die, pier, tier, fur-
rier

RELIGION Relics of an ancient religion are precious.
Did they relinquish their very ancient religion?
Some people relish anything about religion.
Hints: reline, relive, reliable, deli, feline, airline, delicacy

REMEMBER A member should always remember his
club's name.
Remember last December?
Do you remember the Rumba and Samba?
Hints: limber, embers, lumber, slumber, encumber, number,
dumb

REMINISCE Let's reminisce about a lovely scene.
A scent can cause one to reminisce.
We can reminisce as we ascend the stairs.

Hints: scenario, scepter, accept, ascetic, facet, cedar, price

REPRESENT Cain's present will represent his thoughtfulness.
Present laws represent the people's wishes.
If the vice-president is not available, who will represent our president?

Hints: resent, preset, preside, presence, preserve, resign

RHYTHM Some hymns have more rhythm than others.
Rhythm and rhyme are useful to songwriters.
The Rhodesian natives have natural rhythm.

Hints: rhomboid, rhubarb, Rhode Island, rhododendron, rhizome

RIGHT The bright light was right.
h)   You will do it right if you're bright.
Albert might sight them on the right.

Hints: bight, fight, wight, plight, slight, tight, fright

RITE Flying a kite is not a rite.
h)   Let me cite an unusual rite.
The rite occurred at this site.

Hints: bite, sprite, write, mite, item, iterate, pyrite, quite

ROAD Which road did the toad follow?
h)   Will the road take that load?
The jungle is encroaching on the road.

Hints: goad, goal, goat, hoard, coach, roach, poach, goatee

RODE Sam rode his palomino in a new mode.
h)   Alma rode in the local rodeo.
Jim strode while Margaret rode.

Hints: bode, code, lode, ode, commode, model, yodel, node

ROE I love salmon roe, Joe.
h)   The doe did not eat the roe.
  Did Moe or Poe like roe?
Hints: foe, hoe, toe, woe, co-efficient, Oedipus, Chloe

ROOT He hid the loot near a root.
h)   Jane's tooth needed a root canal job.
  His tight boot was at the root of his foot problems.
Hints: soot, toot, scoot, moot, hoop, sloop, hoot, coot

ROUTE Which route will take us out of the woods?
h)   The short route was about a mile away.
  I doubt the scout will find us on this route.
Hints: rout, grout, grouse, loud, louver, outermost, bout,
  sprout

ROW Tow the boat to the end of the row.
h)   Wow, what a row!
  Now, you're starting to row in a circle.
Hints: vow, low, cow, dowry, how, mow, sow, bow,
  scow, trowel

SAFETY Fear was expressed for their safety.
  The cafe provided safety from the rain.
  The precious wafer was brought to safety.
Hints: fete, fetish, fetch, fetid, afeared, fettle,
  fetter

SCENE There wasn't a gene on the scene.
h)   What an obscene scene!
  Oscar was at the scene of the crime.
Hints: scented, center, recent, convene, scenery, epicene

SCENT Perfume is costly even though cent is in the
h)   word scent.
  A recent oil spill left a heavy scent.
  The cooking oil scent at the bicentennial was over-
  whelming.
Hints: ascent, scepter, century, schedule, school, scenic,
  recent

SCHEDULE The school schedule followed the rule.
Our scheme did not fit into the schedule.
Tim's schooner did not arrive on schedule.
Hints: scholar, scholastic, schist, schnook, schism, schizoid, scherzo

SCIENCE A conscience is important in science.
Jake used a scissor for his new science project.
The mouse scurried out of the science room cage.
Hints: scene, scion, scimitar, scissortail, scientific, scilla

SEA Do they have peas across the sea?
h)   Will they serve tea at sea?
Did you hear him say, "Head out to sea"?
Hints: bead, rear, lea, wear, fear, gear, sear, tear, bear

SEAM Did the beam burst its seam?
h)   Ted will sew the seam on the team's banner.
There was a break in a seam on the steamer.
Hints: dream, ream, squeamish, stream, creak, streak, steak

SEE Did anyone see the bee?
h)   A new fee, I see.
I see a steed feeding on weeds.
Hints: wee, heed, veer, deed, steer, tee, glee, tree, free

SEED Don't plant the seed near a weed.
h)   The reed grew from a wee seed.
Sally will feed some seed to her bird.
Hints: heed, steed, need, creed, breed, deed, queen, queer, leer

SEEM You seem to think it will teem soon.
h)   It did seem queer.
The Greek fighter will seem as strong as steel.
Hints: esteem, preen, eel, feel, seep, deep, steep, sleep, deed

SEEN I have seen unfinished steel.
h)   Had you seen her peel the banana?
     That girl has seen an eel.
Hints: been, preen, queen, teen, screen, seed, seep, peen,
     green

SEIZE Seize the boat on the Seine!
     Let's seize the old seismic charts.
     Did they seize Einstein?
Hints: seizure, leisure, lei, seignior, seismometer, seizor

SENSE I sense a tense situation.
h)   A recompense would make sense.
     Their offense makes no sense.
Hints: dense, incense, tension, rinse, lens, pensive, expen-
     sive

SENT The crew went where it was sent.
     They sent the tent to Ghent.
     When was the rent sent?
Hints: dent, cent, lent, fluent, represent, present, resent,
     anent

SEPARATE How do they separate Karate fighters?
     A separate dispatch was sent to Paradise.
     Each class heard a separate parable.
Hint: disparity, parade, para, paragon, parasite, paragraph

SERGEANT Our sergeant had an ant on his serge pants.
     A sergeant has no servant.
     My sergeant meant to kill the serpent.
Hints: wean, lean, year, dean, sermon, serious, serial,
     series

SEVERAL An era usually covers several years.
     Vera has designed several new items.
     Erase several words in your long essay.
Hints: opera, herald, general, eradicate, severance, severable

SEW Barbara will sew a new dress.

h)   I have to sew a few hems on my skirts.

Who will sew a new cushion for the first pew?

Hints: stew, chew, grew, threw, dew, hew, yew, sewer, strew

SHEPHERD The shepherd tends his herd.

A gopher annoyed the shepherd.

What shepherd is near a phone?

Hints: phobia, alphabet, phase, photo, sophomore, Aphrodite

SHOE Maggie scraped her shoe with a hoe.

h)   This shoe pinches my toe.

Some poet wrote a poem about a shoe.

Hints: doe, foe, throe, Chloe, Poe, roe, coed, Oedipus, Joe

SHOO Shoo! Don't bother me too.

h)   A ''choochoo'' train will also shoo animals from the track.

Shoo the pigeons off the roof.

Hints: moon, noon, soon, spoon, woo, food, good, hood, stood

SIGHT His sight fails him in this light.

h)   Land was in sight last night.

She cries at the sight of a fight.

Hints: might, right, straight, tight, plight, slight, bight

SIGN Sign for my raise or I will resign.

h)   Design a sign to read ''No Trespassing''.

Did you sign a check for the ensign?

Hints: consign, ignore, ignite, ignorant, signature, reign

SINE Sine is a mathematical term not a line.

h)   Your answer for the sine is fine.

Sine rhymes with spine.

Hints: mine, nine, tine, vine, wine, pine, dine, equine, shine

SITE It was an excellent site; did the buyer bite?
h)   What a site for kite flying!
   A good site was one item on their list.
Hints: mite, quite, reiterate, sprite, biter, rite, suite,

SO You look so short next to her.
h)   So go on home!
   Harpo was not so funny as a solo.
Hints: polo, cello, hello, bolo, Pluto, hobo, auto, concerto, loco

SOLD Susan sold her old car for gold.
h)   Hold the lease until the house is sold.
   Your father will scold you if you've sold the folder.
Hints: cold, mold, told, behold, bold, Harold, old, wold, uphold

SOLED The shoemaker soled all the shoes with holes.
h)   A caseworker doled out some newly-soled shoes.
   Cole will dole out the soled shoes.
Hints: mole, pole, oleo, solemn, role, oleander, cajole, console

SON Don, is this your oldest son?
h)   My son won a Honda.
   Did I hear your son sing a song in the gondola?
Hints: pond, long, strong, gong, done, tone, bonbon, Congo, bongo

SOPHOMORE The sophomore wanted more photos.
   Does the sophomore drink any homogenized milk?
   Is there a homonym for the word sophomore?
Hints: photostat, homey, homogeny, photogenic, phonograph, phone

SOURCE The source of the force was unknown.

Larceny was not the source of Marcel's problem.

I perceived that the parcel was a source of contention.

Hints: coerce, fierce, surcease, pierce, Circe, Barcelona, tierce

SPEECH Speed up your speech.

My speech will be about a beech tree.

Let's peek at his speech.

Hints: peel, keel, leech, spleen, green, reel, screen, peer, screech

SPONSOR Will you be my sponsor or not?

I am the sponsor for the fair.

Their sponsor demands another sensor.

Hints: sort, sorghum, monitor, tailor, sailor, tonsorial

STATIONARY All was stationary; nary a twig moved.

h)   Be wary of a stationary figure.

That armadillo became stationary when he saw me.

Hints: notary, dictionary, scary, Gary, capillary, ordinary, vary

STATIONERY My stationery is very pretty.

h)   Cheery stationery will gladden the reader.

Good stationery is wasted on a scribbler.

Hints: fernery, trickery, celery, loner, boner, query, onerous

STRAIGHT It was a straight eight.

h)   The trail seemed straight in that light.

Were you afraid the rail might not be straight?

Hints: strain, strait, train, rain, raise, raisin, trace

STRAIT Wait at the strait.

h)   Our traitor escaped through the strait.

At the Strait of Gibraltar, our waiter dropped his tray.

Hints: gait, laity, ait, Kuwait, gaiter, baiter, Tait, trait, wait

STRENGTH Strength means strong.
   Length and strength can be important factors.
   Lengthen the rope and thicken it for extra strength.
Hints: string, strong, strengthen, estrange, astringent,
   Ringo

SUBSTANTIAL Substantial evidence is often only par-
tial evidence.
   That Prudential building is quite substantial.
   Your credentials are substantial.
Hints: essential, torrential, confidential, potential, tiara

SUBTLE The stubble of his beard was subtle.
   No battle is subtle.
   Subtle is the same as subtitle without the IT.
Hints: bottle, obstacle, brittle, scuttle, subtlety, shuttle
Note: A variation seldom used is SUTTLE.

SUITE It is quite a grand suite.
h)   The fruit ruined the couch in the new suite.
   My suitcase was placed in the wrong suite.
Hints: suitor, cuisine, quit, bruin, suing, pursuing, recruit

SUN Will the sun toast a bun?
h)   June said, "It's one hundred degrees in the sun."
   I don't like to run in the sun.
Hints: pun, lung, fun, spun, tunnel, funnel, stun, lunge

SUPPOSE Suppose I oppose her?
   Let's suppose they topple the ruler.
   How do you suppose the guppy got out of the bowl?
Hints: mapped, wrapped, capped, supped, apple, grapple,
   ripple

SURPRISE The new fur coat was a surprise.
   Any surplus will be a surprise.
   Our treasure surprise was a turkey.
Hints: purpose, usurp, burp, cur, occur, curtain, durable,
   leisure

SUSPENSE Movie suspense can be intense.
There was no recompense after the suspense.
This book starts with tense suspense.
Hints: dense, incense, sense, opens, rinse, lens, pensive

SWEET A bird's tweet can be sweet.
h)   Did you meet that sweet girl?
Do you smell the sweet flowers on this street?
Hints: discreet, beet, creed, feet, teeter, week, weevil

SYMBOL A bold symbol will be seen.
h)   The boll weevil could be used as a symbol.
That symbol on his bolo is interesting.
Hints: gambol, bolt, bologna, colt, hold, cold, sold, gold

SYNONYMOUS Her pseudonym is synonymous with a
color.
Harmony and melody are clearly synonymous.
Symbol is not synonymous with cymbal.
Hints: homonym, antonym, rhyme, synonym, nymph,
symphony,

TAIL Any cat will wail if it loses its tail.
h)   Gail hit the quail's tail.
Which dog's tail landed in a paint pail?
Hints: sail, mail, hail, rail, ail, snail, bail, daily, fail

TALE Would you like to hear a tale about a whale?
h)   Is this tale for sale?
Did you hear the tale about the gale at Yale?
Hints: ale, bale, dale, pale, stale, talent, kale, male, scale

TARE Take care to get a very accurate tare.
h)   Don't dare to include the tare.
Tare and rare have the word are in them.
Hints: bare, fare, hare, mare, rare, stare, snare, pare, glare

TEAR (1) Will you wear it with a tear?
h)   Will the bear tear the parcel?

Did you hear something tear?

Hints: pear, year, fear, rear, gear, dear, near, sear, dreary
(See TEAR 2 below.)

TEAR (2) A tear appeared in her eye.

h)   Clear the tear from your eye.
Remembrance of last year's reunion caused a tear to form.

Hints: sear, dear, pear, gear, smear, spear, ear, fear, hear

TENDENCY There was a tendency toward dependency.
Our teacher had a tendency toward leniency.
His family had a tendency toward corpulency.

Hints: congruency, frequency, diligency, fraudulency

THAN Ann is shorter than John.

h)   Is a woman more sensitive than a man?
Dan can tan better on a boat than on sand.

Hints: land, ban, pan, ran, an, hand, shank, tank, bank, rank

THEIR Their aunt is coming to visit her new heir.

h)   Their heir is nine days old.
Eire is their home land.

Hints: Eir, Eireannach, Weir, stein, vein, rein, reirrigate

THEMSELVES The elves themselves made the toys.
The boys made two bookshelves by themselves.
They were twelve themselves once.

Hints: delves, helves, ourselves, selvage (or selvedge), pelvis

THEN When you arrive, then we will sing.

h)   A hen lays an egg; then we eat it.
By then, Ben's shenanigan was a phenomenon.

Hints: earthen, tend, bend, send, mend, hence, henna, Henry, hennery

THERE We went from here to there in ten minutes.
h)   We'll be there soon; it's merely a mile.
   Will it adhere there?
Hints: sphere, austere, insincere, where, revere, persevere,
   interfere

THEY'RE (THEY ARE) They're (They are) going to
h)   meet her at the station.
   Do you know if they're (they are) interested?
   They're (They are) wonderful parents.
Hints: (See words in parentheses for clarification.)

THOROUGH It was a thorough exam for that borough.
   Thorpe performed a thorough inspection.
   The thoroughbred had a thorough workout.
Hints: thorn, Thorold, Thor, horoscope, thorax, thorough-
   fare

THOSE My nose is sensitive to those tissues.
   Those people chose to pose.
   Are those girls nosey!
Hints: close, lose, arose, rose, hose, expose,
   suppose

THOUGHT I thought that I had bought a blue dress.
   Jim thought that he had caught a fish.
   Angie thought it was a wrought iron chair.
Hints: eight, weight, haughty, tight, light, ought, fought

THREW The crew threw a line to the victim.
h)   She threw a new book at him.
   Lewis threw a few balls to his son.
Hints: grew, drew, dew, sew, yew, shrew, brew, hew,
   view, blew

THROUGH The victims suffered through the rough
h)   treatment.
   It was tough going through the blizzard.
   The baker cut a hole through the doughnut dough.

Hints: cough, bough, fought, thought, bought, wrought, sought

TIER The bier was on the top tier, stacked on the pier.
h)   Our neighbor's chandelier has more than one tier of prisms.
   The group arrived at the pier earlier than we did.
Hints: frontier, chevalier, cavalier, grenadier, cashier

TO Will you come to play today?
h)   Does this pendulum go to and fro?
   The hobo went to the Rialto.
Hints: ditto, coco, Apollo, Como, dodo, staccato, allegro, bolo

TOGETHER When can we get together again?
   Do you know whether or not they will get together?
   Rosie and Roger saw the geyser together.
Hints: tether, ether, bellwether, blether, Ethel, nether, seether

TOO Too much sugar is bad for a tooth.
h)   We saw a cockatoo at the zoo too.
   Their baby enjoyed playing peekaboo too.
Hints: soon, boon, raccoon, Roo, woo, zoology, shampoo, taboo

TRAGEDY The tragedy created rage.
   A tragic mistake can cause a tragedy.
   The old stage was used for the tragedy.
Hints: agent, agenda, sage, ageratum, age-old, page, badger

TRANSFERRED The car was transferred by ferry.
   After they conferred, they transferred the ferret.
   Ann was transferred because she erred too often.
Hints: ferrite, referred, deferred, preferred, terrible

TRIED Jean tried to save her plant but it died.
They diversified and tried to save the business.
The young girl tried to look dignified for the interview.
Hints: fortified, fried, unified, petrified, tied, gratified, spied

TRIES Tom always tries to make French fries.
Ada tries to make perfect pies.
Alf pries and tries to collect gossip.
Hints: dignifies, signifies, ties, unifies, diversifies, Aries, dries

TWO Twins are two of a kind.
h)   Two stars will twinkle brighter than one.
A two-fold door has two parts.
Hints: work, worn, worm, world, two-way, two-by-four, two-bit

UNDOUBTEDLY You undoubtedly know Ted Ly.
Undoubtedly, that news had been reported earlier.
Now, they will undoubtedly be deported.
Hints: ousted, sorted, united, excited, sighted, lighted, bed

USE You abuse your body if you use too much alcohol.
h)   I will use this one because it's blue.
Does it confuse you when I use the translation?
Hints: excuse, fuse, muse, ruse, accuse, amuse, grouse, rouse

VACUUM Using a vacuum can become humdrum.
Don't rely on a continuum from a vacuum.
A peculiarity of that word vacuum is its double U.
Hints: succumb, pendulum, numb, auditorium, aquarium, unplumb

VIEW Did your view include the pier?
Vie for a seat with a better view.
Can you get a view of Aries?
Hints: science, pie, brie, diet, review, lie, Juliet, anxiety

WAIT I will plait your hair if you wait.

h)   Wait for me; slow your gait.
First you bait; then you wait.

Hints: faith, ait, wraith, laity, waiter, strait, trait, Tait

WAY Okay, let's go this way.

h)   Kay did not say much along the way.
Each will pay his own way.

Hints: ray, cay, day, stay, bay, hay, lay, May, Fay, blue-jay, gray

WEAR Brenda will wear last year's bathing suit.

h)   Do not tear that dress; I plan to wear it soon.
Shall I wear a fancy earring?

Hints: clear, sear, hear, rear, spear, bear, ear, pear, dear

WEATHER Our weatherman predicts more heat.

h)   A leather jacket is good weather protection.
The cool weather gave us a breather.

Hints: treat, wheat, seat, seal, heather, breath, beat, feat, neat

WEIGH Weigh the package before eight.

h)   My neighbor doesn't like to weigh herself.
How much would that sleigh weigh?

Hints: weigher, weighty, neigh, inveigh, outweigh, sleight, Leigh

WEIGHT For his height, he carries a lot of weight at the
h)   office.
The baby's weight is eight pounds.
His sleight of hand changed the scale weight.

Hints: neigh, sleigh, neighbor, overweight, inveigh, eighteen

WEIRD It was a weird day for the new heir.
Their dog is weird.
Fishing with a weir is weird.

Hints: Eire, heirloom, stein, vein, rein, feint, Seine, skein

WHERE Where are we going from here?

h)   There is where he went.

Wherever he goes that's where trouble will follow.

Hints: they, whey, anywhere, whew, what, which, who, when

WHETHER Allen doesn't know whether to go or stay

h)   with Heather.

The pickle will whet my appetite whether I eat it or not.

I will go to the class whether you go there or not.

Hints: whence, where, when, which, who, what, whew, wheel

WHO'S (WHO IS) I know who's (who is) the best reader.

h)   Who's (Who is) coming to the party?

Did they announce who's (who is) to be the valedictorian?

Hints: (See words in parentheses for clarification).

WHOLE Agnes read the whole book while we were gone.

h)   Who ate the whole cake?

The word hole is in the word whole; add W for the whole word.

Hints: whose, whom, why, whopper, whoa, whoopee, wholesome

WHOSE Whose class do you think will lose?

h)   Do you know whose house this is?

Whose spouse is most thoughtful?

Hints: chose, those, douse, hose, grouse, rouse, close, rose

WOMAN Woman was created from man.

A Roman woman wore sandals.

Stan ran toward the van.

Hints: pan, ban, can, Dan, fan, hand, land, sand, tan, wan, Nan

WON I wonder if they've won one game.

h)   Alma won the tennis tournament with a wonderful score.

Bernice won a box of bonbons.

Hints: ton, son, yon, don, gone, wondrous, wonder, wont, won't

WRIGHT The wright did his woodworking the right way.
h)   A mystery playwright must create the right situation.
   A wright will probably avoid hightest equipment.
Hints: hightail, high, tide, wringer, fright, bright, light

WRITE Cite the circumstances when you write your letter.
h)   Write your name on the kite.
   When you write a letter, you reunite with a friend.
Hints: spite, despite, invite, excite, sprite, recite, nitrite

YEWS A woodsman hews yews.
h)   Sometimes yews are felled by crews.
   A grinder spews chips of yews.
Hints: stews, reviews, sews, news, mew, blew, drew, grew, pew

YIELD Yield the field!
   A knight did yield his shield.
   Katherine would not yield her purse to the thief.
Hints: relief, grief, believe, wield, diet, diem, Sadie, brie

YORE The knights of yore wore suits of armor.
h)   Some tales of yore were filled with gore.
   I love to pore over tales of yore.
Hints: bore, core, adore, more, fore, tore, store, folklore

YOUR Your garden is prettier than our garden.
h)   Come to our house for your nap.
   Your courage was inspiring.
Hints: sour, four, pour, tour, dour, glamour, amour, scour

YOU'RE (YOU ARE) Tell me when you're (you are)
h)   finished.
   A life can be ruined if you're (you are) a drug addict.
   You're (You are) the most popular girl in your school.
Hints: (See words in parentheses for clarification.)

A Few Basic
Spelling Rules

IE or EI?

The letter I usually precedes the letter E <u>except</u> when used after the letter C. After the letter C, the letter I follows the letter E.

This rule has many exceptions. If the sound created is an A, then EI is usually used.

EXAMPLES: weigh, neighbor, reign weight, eight, inveigle, neigh

OTHER EXCEPTIONS: leisure, weird, seize, height, foreign

Plurals

Plurals are not created by adding 'S.

EXAMPLES: hats not hat's, books not book's

Numbers, letters, symbols and figures use 'S to denote a plural.

EXAMPLES: l's, p's and q's

Plurals of Words Ending in Y

For words ending in Y, change the Y to I and add ES.

EXCEPTIONS: If the Y is preceded by a vowel, do not change spelling. Keep the Y and add an S.

EXAMPLES: key keys, donkey donkeys, monkey monkeys

If ending to be added starts with an I (ex. -ing), do not drop or change Y.

Apostrophe

Omission of Letters An apostrophe is used where there is an omission of one or more letters.

EXAMPLES: can't = cannot, it's = it is, hasn't = has not

Possession The apostrophe is also used to show possession.

EXAMPLES: Singular-the man's son = son of the man

Plural-When words already end in S, just add an apostrophe. girls' teacher = teacher of the girls

Plural and Collective Nouns-If a word means more than one, add apostrophe and S. women's, men's, group's

Proper Names-When proper names end in S add an apostrophe only. An extra S may be added if it will not create an awkward series of sounds.

Compound Words-In compound words, the last part of the compound uses the sign of possession. father-in-law's

Joint Possessive-When two or more persons own the same thing, add apostrophe and S to the second (or last) person's name. Albert and Susie's house. (They own the house together.)

Individual Possessive (more than one is mentioned)-When each person owns something, use apostrophe and an S for each person's name. Albert's and Susan's cars (They each own their own car.)

Double Possessive-When two ownerships are mentioned, use the word "of" with the first and an apostrophe and S with the second. the friend of my cousin's book not my cousin's friend's book

Hyphenation

If two words are used as an adjective or verb with one meaning, they are usually hyphenated.

EXAMPLE: conscience-stricken, well-equipped, lace-trimmed

EXCEPTIONS: When one word ends in -LY. comparatively easy, barely done, rarely seen

Compound Nouns and Numbers

Nouns: It's best to refer to a dictionary.

Numbers: From twenty-one through ninety-nine are hyphenated.

Double Consonants

As a rule, consonants are doubled after short vowels. Some consonants are frequently doubled (F, L, S, C,). Double C becomes CK.

EXCEPTIONS: Some consonants are never doubled. (H, J, Q, V, W, X)

Final Silent E

If a word ends in a silent E, keep the E when adding an ending that starts with a consonant.

EXAMPLES: loose loosely, use useful, bare barely, comparative comparatively

Prefixes

(Selected because they are trouble makers.)

per	=	through	pre	=	before
anti	=	against	ante	=	before
de	=	from or down	di	=	twice

Word Endings

-ents   -ants
These are usually plural endings.
EXAMPLES: pres<u>ents</u>, oppon<u>ents</u>, experim<u>ents</u>, confid<u>ants</u>, serge<u>ants</u>,

-ence   -ance
These are endings for abstract nouns.
EXAMPLES: pres<u>ence</u>, emin<u>ence</u>, resid<u>ence</u>, confid<u>ence</u>, ro-
mance, enh<u>ance</u>, dist<u>ance</u>, radi<u>ance</u>

-ible   Use when word would be incomplete without suffix.
EXAMPLE: sensible, SENS is incomplete without -IBLE

-able   Usually end of word that is complete without suffix.
EXAMPLES: answerable ANSWER, readable READ, break-
able BREAK (All are complete without ending.)

-ar   (least commonly used)
EXAMPLES: calend<u>ar</u>, st<u>ar</u>, popul<u>ar</u>, globul<u>ar</u>, gramm<u>ar</u>, modul<u>ar</u>

-or   (the common ending)
EXAMPLES: spons<u>or</u>, indicat<u>or</u>, rot<u>or</u>, doct<u>or</u>, janit<u>or</u>, sail<u>or</u>

-er   (indicates occupation)
EXAMPLES: bak<u>er</u>, teach<u>er</u>, buy<u>er</u>, shoemak<u>er</u>, butch<u>er</u>, trad<u>er</u>,
sell<u>er</u>

-cede   (the common form)
EXAMPLES: con<u>cede</u>, pre<u>cede</u>, re<u>cede</u>

-ceed   (three words end this way)
EXAMPLES: ex<u>ceed</u>, suc<u>ceed</u>, pro<u>ceed</u>, (<u>not</u> procedure)

-sede   (only used in one word)
EXAMPLE: super<u>sede</u>

Word Groups

Unusual Spelling

Look up words alphabetically in this book. If suggestions offered do not help, try to find your own trick for remembering spelling.

Letters Not Pronounced

(Underlined)

acquaint
acquaintance
acquire
aisle
answer
bouillon
condemn
discipline
dealt
favorite
foreign
guarantee

hors d'oeuvres
length
maneuver
psychology
reign
rhythm
reminisce
schedule
strength
subtle
thorough
vacuum

Some Odd Spellings

efficient (IE after C)
fulfill (one L then two)
height (EI not after C)
liaison (three vowels together,
A is between two I's)
parallel (two L's then one L)
weird (EI not after C)

Homonyms

These words sound alike but are usually spelled differently.

aisle	cede	feat	isle	no
isle	seed	feet	I'll	know
I'll			aisle	
	cent	flew		one
ate	scent	flue	it's	won
eight	sent		its	
		for		our
bare	cents	fore	knew	hour
bear	sense	four	new	
			gnu	pail
beer	cite	forth		pale
bier	sight	fourth	know	
	site		no	pair
blew		gnu		pare
blue	cymbal	knew	lead	pear
	symbol	new	(metal)	
board				passed
bored	dear	grate	led	past
	deer	great		
bouillon			made	peace
bullion	desert	hay	maid	piece
	dessert	hey		
brake			mail	phase
break	eight	hear	male	faze
	ate	here		
bread			meat	pore
bred	faze	hole	meet	pour
	phase	whole	mete	
canvas				principal
canvass	fair	hour	new	principle
	fare (noun)	our	gnu	
	fare (verb)		knew	

rain	scent	sign	tear	weather
reign	sent	sine	tier	whether
	cent			
read		sold	than	whole
red	sea	soled	then	hole
	see			
read		son	their	whose
reed	seam	sun	there	who's
	seem		they're	
real		stationary		won
reel	seed	stationery	threw	one
	cede		through	
right		straight		wright
rite	sense	strait	to	write
wright	cents		too	right
write		suite	two	rite
	sew	sweet		
road	so		use	yews
rode		symbol	yews	use
	shoe	cymbal		
roe	shoo		wait	yore
row		tail	weight	you're
	sight	tale		your
root	site		way	
route	cite	tare	weigh	
		tear		
scene			wear	
seen			where	

Test Yourself

To find out what you have learned, select the words which are spelled accurately in the sentences below. Write the correct spelling on a separate piece of paper. (Words are alphabetically arranged in case you just want to check a few words.) The answers are on pages 85 through 87.

Will your car (accomodate, acomodate, accommodate) six people comfortably?

I chose not to (acustom, accostum, accustom) myself to the habit of smoking.

Did he (achieve, acheive, acheeve) his goal?

May I (accquaint, acquaint, aquaint) you with Mary Lu?

James was only an (acquaintance, aquaintance, accquaintance).

Should I (aquire, acquire, accquire) another friend?

The (actual, atual, aktual) cost was higher than expected.

Giving (advise, advize, advice) can be awkward.

(Advice, Advize, Advise) your neighbors to lock their doors.

Any (effect, affect, afect) on the situation may be minimal.

Lean (against, agenst, aginst) the door if it sticks.

Some theatres have more than one (isle, ile, aisle).

A hug can mean (alot, allot, a lot) to a child.

(Amung, Among, Ammong) the crowd were three actors.

What (amownt, amount, amont) did he pay for the tickets?

The (analysis, analisis, analisys) showed no malignancy.

They must (analise, analyze, analize) the results at once!

Don't (answer, anser, ansur) me in that tone!

Was the change (aparent, aparunt, apparent) to the group?

Let's (appreciate, apreciate, appresiate) our good health.

(Approch, Approach, Approoch) from the side of the building.

The (aproximate, approximate, aproxamite) time is 9:30 A. M.

My (arthritis, arthuritis, artritus) has been killing me.

I read an interesting (articul, articol, article) in the Reader's Digest.

Jane's dog (eight, ate) all of the small steaks.

An (athlete, athalete, atlete) wins awards if he trains well.

Mother Hubbard's cupboards were (bear, bare, bair).

Please don't feed the (bare, bair, bear).

Light (beer, bier, bere) is popular today.

The corpse was placed in his (bier, beer, bere) yesterday.

Little Bobbie (blue, blew) out his two birthday candles.

(Blue, Blew) skies appear in many paintings.

Use the wooden (bord, board, bored) as a second shelf.

She was (bored, bord, board) by the long lecture.

(Bullion, Bouillon) is a very pleasant beginning for a meal.

Step on the (break, brake) right now!

(Bread, Bred) and butter are a good snack combination.

Careful, or you'll (break, brake) the cut glass bowl.

The horses were (bread, bred) in Virginia by one of my dear friends.

A piece of gold (bouillon, bullion) can be very heavy.

Jim's (business, bisness, bizness) was not failing.

Is a bee always (busy, bisy, bizy)?

(Canvass, Canvis, Canvas) is a very sturdy cloth.

Did they (canvas, canvis, canvass) every house on the street?

A tightrope walker must be extremely (carful, careful, cairful).

Sloppy writing is just plain (carless, cairless, careless).

Which new (catigory, catagory, category) do you prefer?

Will you (sede, seed, cede) the election today?

I won't give a (sent, cent) more this time.

Fifty (cents, sents, sense) was a fair price for the book.

Are you (sertin, certain, certen) this is the right road?

(Chief, Cheef, Cheif) Three Feathers led the pow–wow yesterday.

What other (choice, choise) did she have left?

(Choose, Chose) between the two grey suits.

George (chose, choose) to break the latest rules.

Can you (site, cite) any other court case?

Susie's (cloths, clothes, clowthes) are always chic.

It was a (comparative, comparetive, comparitive) situation.

Don't (condem, condemn, cundemn) him without a trial.

Will your (conscience, concience, consceince) bother you?

Always be (consientious, conscientious, consceinsious) about your work.

Joseph was (conscious, concius, conscius) during his operation.

(Concider, Consider, Consiter) the other person's feelings.

There was a (continuus, continius, continuous) line of people around the building.

A buyer's (convenience, convineinse, conveniense) should be considered when planning a house.

Most people do not like (critisism, criticizm, criticism).

Some neighbors like to (critisize, criticize, critisise) the work of others.

Did (curiosity, coriosity, curiocity) really kill a cat?

Aren't you (curious, corious, curius) about the test results?

A new (corriculum, curiculm, curriculum) will be started.

The dancer dropped her (symbol, cymbal, simbol) as she twirled.

The cards (dealed, delt, dealt) by the dealer didn't help the gambler.

"(Dear, Deer) Becky," is a good beginning for a personal letter.

Look at the tiny (dier, dear, deer) at the edge of the lake!

Being (dependent, dependint, dependont) on another can be very restricting.

(Dessert, Desert) living differs from urban living.

Her (desireability, desirability, disiribility) was marred by her sloppy appearance.

(Disire, Desire, Deseire) can lead to disaster.

The unemployed laborer left the office in (dispair, despair).

(Desert, Dessert) is the best part of the meal.

Any (diference, difference, differance) in color would be noticeable.

Tim's sneakers were (diferent, different, differant) from Luke's.

Don't (disapoint, disappoint, desappoint) me, be prompt.

It was a (disastrous, disasdrous, disastrus) accident for the bus company.

Teachers must (discipline, disipline, descipline) unruly students frequently.

A contagious (desease, disease, diseese) can spread quickly.

Ice cream can be (divine, devine, davine) with the extra trimmings.

His stain was the (affect, effect) of careless painting.

The European trains are (afficient, efficient, ifficient); they are always on time.

(Eight, Ate) children in one family creates a lot of work for the mother.

Amy did not want to (embaras, embarrass, embarass) you.

Sam's new (equipment, equipement, equiment) was missing.

Each car was (equipt, equiped, equipped) with an air bag.

Be polite to the guests, (especially, specialy, especialy) the guest of honor.

Wanda tends to (exaggerate, exagerate, exajerate) her sizes.

Achieving (exellence, excellance, excellence) is the goal of an athlete.

Paul's grades were always (excellent, exellent, excelent).

The (exitable, excitible, excitable) chickens were frightened by the train passing nearby.

Diet and (esercise, exercise, exercize) are important to one's health.

Extra trimmings can mean extra (expense, espense, expenze).

They say (esperience, experiance, experience) is the best teacher.

A scientist must (experiment, expiriment, experament) to find a solution.

(Explination, Esplanation, Explanation) of a problem can sometimes lead to an understanding.

His injury was (extremely, estremely, extremly) painful.

The (fair, fare) maiden liked the tall, dark-haired lad.

What is the (fare, fair) on the train to Chicago?

Did they (fair, fare) well as a result of the legal procedure?

Movies stars (fasinate, fascinate, fescinate) many people.

Do you have a (favorit, favorete, favorite) candy recipe?

Your accusations do not (faze, fase, phase) me at all.

Sky-diving is quite a treacherous (feet, feat).

Bunions disfigure a person's (feat, feet).

(Fictious, Fictitious, Fictisious) stories are popular with children.

Daisies in a (field, feeld, feild) are a welcome sight.

The plane (flue, flew) at an altitude of 35,000 feet.

A clean (flew, flue) will permit a better air flow.

This gift is (fore, for, four) your anniversary.

"(For, Four, Fore)!" shouted the impatient golfer.

Our products are exported to many (forein, forin, foreign) countries.

Some clocks have pendulums that move back and (forth, fourth).

Esther is now over (fourty, forty, forety) years old.

As we move (foreward, fourward, forward) along the line, more people are joining the end of the line.

Some flowers have only (fore, four, for) petals.

On the (forth, fourth, foreth) day, the heat wave ended.

Here comes my (friend, freind, frend), Daisy.

Can you (fullfill, fullfil, fulfill) all the entrance requirements?

The (fundemental, fundamental, fundimental) problem was obviously his manner of treating others.

Was there a (new, gnu) at that old zoo?

(Grammer, Grammar, Gramma) is not easy for some students to learn.

Adjust the height of the fireplace (great, grate) a little.

I feel so (great, grate) after my spectacular vacation.

A (garanty, guarantee, garranty) is usually helpful in a dispute.

(Guidence, Guidance, Guidense) counsellors are used in high schools to guide the students in their choice of subjects.

John was (guiding, gideing, guideing) us along the path when we saw the tarantula.

Last week we went for a long (hey, hay) ride to the lake.

Can you (hear, here) the little wren singing in the backyard?

Additional (hight, height, hite) can be an advantage in a crowd.

(Hear, Here) comes the circus parade, right on time this year!

(Hay, Hey)! stop running around the pool; you'll slip and hurt yourself.

The workmen dug the (whole, hole, hoal) in the wrong place.

(Ors d'urves, Or d'erves, Hors d'oeuvres) are a tasty treat.

At what (our, hour) shall I arrive next Wednesday morning?

That (huge, hug, huje) tree was just struck by lightning.

When you're (hungree, hungry, hongry), heat the soup.

(Ignorence, Ignorance, Ignoranse) can lead to problems.

(I'll, Isle, Ile) meet you at home after the fashion show.

Nowadays, no one is (indespensible, indispensable, indispensabel).

(Influentiel, Influential, Influencial) people can usually get their wishes fulfilled.

Your excuses do not (intrest, interist, interest) me at all.

Must you always (interfere, interfer, interfear) with my endeavors?

Can you (interpret, interpre, intirpret) the hieroglyphics?

Debra's (interpretation, interpratation, interpiration) of the regulations was incorrect.

If I (interupt, interrupt, intarupt) you, you'll be annoyed.

The suggestion was (irrelent, irrelevant, irrelevent) to the problem.

A Hawaiian (aisle, isle, ile) is a peaceful, beautiful sight.

(Its, It's) a shame the bridle path in the park is closed.

Each zebra has (it's, its) own stripe pattern.

Everyone (knew, new, gnu) about the secret door and room.

Do you (no, know) where the canary has flown to?

(Nowlege, Knowledge, Knoledge) is a must in these times.

The (Labur, Labor, Laber) Party won the election easily.

Larry's (laboratory, laberatory, laveratory) is doing cancer research.

Each (labora, laborer, laberer) received a small wage.

Ceramic tile was (layed, laid, lade) for the kitchen floor.

(Later, Lader, Laider) in the day, we will have a board meeting.

Will you agree to (leed, lead, lede) the graduation march?

Water sitting in a pipe may contain (led, lead).

Eunice (lead, led) the way to the summit without incident.

Rest and (lesure, leisure, liesure) time will relax a tired laborer.

My ruler's (lenth, length, lanthe) is twelve inches, a foot.

(Lenthening, Lengthening, Lenthaning) the curtain rod was not enough.

Let's create a (liaison, liason, laison) between the two new groups.

Ann's (lisense, licence, license) has just expired.

The (likeness, likness, laikness) of one boy to his cousin was uncanny.

Changing the (lojistics, logistecs, logistics) can sometimes solve a problem.

The blue thread was dangling (loose, lose) from his sleeve.

A (loser, looser) corset would be much more comfortable.

Don't (loose, lose) your lunch money again.

The racer felt like a (loser, looser) before the race began.

(Luxery, Luxury, Luxiry) is sought after by many.

Helene (maid, made) a new dress for the wedding reception.

Next week we must hire another live-in (made, maid).

Today's (mail, male) included three large checks.

(Maintinance, Maintenance, Mantenance) of equipment is very important to future production.

The (male, mail) of some species is the more colorful of the mates.

Gloria can execute a fancy (manuver, maneuver, manuever) on skates.

It was her third (mariage, marridge, marriage) to the same man.

(Mathematics, Matthematics, Matematecs) is not an easy subject for everyone.

That's what I (ment, meant) to say but I misspoke.

Tasty (meet, meat, mete) can become a delicious entree.

He doesn't understand the (machanics, mechanics, mecanics) of the toy.

(Medicine, Medcine, Medasin) men were highly revered by their tribesmen.

Grand Central Station is no place to (mete, meet, meat) anyone.

Sarah won the track (meet, meat, mete) two years in a row.

(Mete, Meat, Meet) out all the portions, Lillie.

(Minature, Miniature, Miniture) horses are the size of large dogs.

Imps usually get into (mischif, mischief, mischuff).

Jacob's (narrative, narritave, naritive) was too long and very dull.

It is (necessary, nesessary, nesassery) to have a registration card to vote.

(Knew, Gnu, New) books can be full of pleasant surprises.

Is she really going to be (ninty, ninety) years old tomorrow?

(Know, No) news can be very upsetting to a family.

There is a (noticable, noticeable, noticible) difference between the sisters.

Have you been (noticing, notising, noticeing) any change in color?

My only (obsticle, obstacle, obstecle) was the hole in the road.

When will it (occur, occurr, ocurr) to you to save your money?

The accident (occured, occurred, ocurred) yesterday on Main Street.

Nancy's birth was a surprise (ocurrence, occurrence, occurence).

Both events (occurring, occuring, ocurring) at the same time was a coincidence.

Please (omit, omitt, ommit) the last paragraph of the story.

Has anyone here lost (won, one) brown and white shoe?

Are the new computers easier to (operate, opperate, operat) then the ones we have now?

My (oponent, opponent, opponant) was very tired after the swimming races.

Shall we (oppose, opose, uppose) the new regulations regarding class limitations?

(Optemizm, Optimism, Optamism) can keep one's spirit up.

If you know its (origin, orrigin, origen), please tell us.

An (originel, origenal, original) painting can be expensive.

(Our, Hour) teacher drilled us in spelling each morning.

I'd like a (pare, pair, pear) of stockings, please.

This (pale, pail) holds one gallon of liquid.

Lana's (pail, pale) face needed a little bit of color.

(Parelel, Parallel, Paralel) lines are easy to draw.

Will you (pear, pair, pare) me an orange, please?

Jonathan (passed, past) his algebra test easily.

In the (past, passed), life was much simpler.

The world would be a happier place with (piece, peace).

That large rock is shaped like a (pare, pear).

Can you (percieve, perceive, perceeve) of such an idea?

It was supposed to have been a (permenent, permanent, perminent) repair.

Don't be so (persistent, persistint, persistant) in your demands.

My bedroom contains my (personnel, personal) possessions.

Every (personnel, personal) department is a busy place in these days of high unemployment.

Shall we try to (pursuade, persuade, pirsuade) Janice to change her mind?

Your questions must (pertain, purtain, pertane) to the subject being discussed.

Is this to be used in (faze, phase) one, two or three?

Bert's (filosophy, philosophy, phelosofy) differed from Jay's.

(Physical, Fisical, Physicol) fitness can help prolong a person's life.

That small (peace, piece, peice) of pecan pie will be fine, thank you.

A good (playright, playrite, playwright) needs an active imagination.

At Christmas time, the (pointsettia, poinsettia, pointsetta) is the dominant flower.

Sean's enlarged (pore, pour) is in a very conspicuous place.

Let it (pour, pore) all week long, we need rain badly.

The letter A will always (proceed, precede, preceed) B alphabetically.

Some youths (preferr, prefer, preffer) loud music even though it will affect their hearing ability.

This color is (preferred, prefered, preffered) for the kitchen.

(Prejudise, Pregudice, Prejudice) can lead to much unhappiness.

(Priceing, Pricing, Prising) at a garage sale is mostly guesswork.

Art that is (primitive, primative, premitive) is usually simpler and more basic.

Cary's school (principle, principal, principol) was a very understanding disciplinarian.

You are overlooking a basic (principle, principol, principal) of democracy.

It was our (privelege, privilege, privalege) to meet the king and queen.

Louise followed the correct (precedure, proceedure, procedure) by calling the roll first.

(Proceed, Procede, Prosede) to the nearest exit slowly; the building is on fire.

His height would cause him to be (prominent, promminent, promenent) in an average group.

(Sycology, Psycology, Psychology) is an interesting subject.

Don't (persue, pursue, pirsue) the wrong career or you will always regret it.

What (quantity, qantity, quanity) did he request from you?

(Rein, Rain, Reign, Rane) is beautiful when it's needed.

Always (reed, rede, read) slowly and enunciate carefully.

The name of each book Ed (read, red) is listed in a notebook.

Dolls now look like (reel, real) babies.

Will you (recieve, receive, receeve) the package today?

Some businesses have (receiving, receiveing, recieving) departments.

(Read, Red, Redd) is a warm, almost hot, color.

Were you able to find a book that was suitable to (read, rede, reed)?

David's fishing (reel, real, rele) was badly snarled.

(Refering, Referring, Refurring) to the last paragraph, drop the last sentence.

Queen Elizabeth will (rane, rein, rain, reign) as long as she wishes.

Is Kathleen a (relative, reletive, relitive) of Laura?

(Releive, Relieve, Relive) the pressure and everything will run smoothly.

(Relegin, Religian, Religion) is a touchy topic for discussion.

I can't (remember, remenber, remebber) her last name.

Let's (remenis, reminisce, remenisce) about our childhood; guess I'm getting old.

Does this survey (represent, repersent, reprisent) the whole community?

Good (rhythm, rithym, rythm) helps make a tune popular.

Go to the (rite, right, wright, write) at the next corner.

A (right, write, wright, rite) of passage is very important to some native tribes.

Which is the (road, rode) we're looking for, Linda?

It is written that Lady Godiva (road, rode) a white horse.

Fish (row, roe) are a very special delicacy for some people.

(Rute, Root, Route) out all the tall weeds first!

(Route, Rute, Root) 66 is a very well-known highway.

Can you (row, roe) in a straight line most of the time?

Policemen try to protect the (safty, safety, saffety) of each citizen.

The (sene, scene, seen) in the painting was very relaxing.

The perfume, Chanel #5, has a delicate (scent, sent, cent).

(Scedule, Schedule) my arrival for 5:30 on Tuesday.

Research is very costly when it involves (sience, science).

Sailors spend most of their time at (see, sea).

Paula ripped the (seem, seam, seme) on her shorts when she fell off the dock.

(Sea, See) the huge helicopter crossing the bay?

This (seed, cede, sead) should germinate quickly indoors.

Does it (seem, seam, seme) like fall or spring to you?

Was the ghost (scene, sene, seen) frequently?

(Seize, Seeze, Sieze) the opportunity when it arises!

I could (sence, cents, sense) that she was not ready for the test.

The book will be (scent, sent, cent) by parcel post tomorrow.

(Sepirate, Separate, Seperate) the white from colored clothes.

(Sargent, Sergent, Sergeant) Jones was very strict with the men in his unit.

I'll take (several, severel, severil) spools of this thread.

Arlene learned to (so, sew, sow) hems as a child in Belgium.

Sheep need a (sheepherd, shepherd, sheperd) to care for them.

Please give me a larger (shoo, shoe); this one's too tight.

(Shoe, Shoo)! keep your goat away from me; he smells bad.

(Cite, Site, Sight) and Sound shows are very entertaining.

Please, (sine, sign, syne) next to the X at the bottom.

What is the (sign, sine) of the acute angle?

Select a level (cite, sight, site) for the house.

(Sew, So, Sow), you're late again today.

"(Sold, Soled)!" shouted the auctioneer, striking his podium.

My shoes need to be (sold, soled) in time for the party.

This is my eldest (son, sun), Alexander.

Next year, Margaret will be a (sophomore, sofomore, sophemore) in high school.

One (sorce, sourse, source) of energy is the sun.

The mayor's (speach, speech, spiech) was very short but clever.

You need a (sponsor, sponser, sponcer) to enter the contest.

A (stationery, stationary, stationiry) object is easier to hit than a moving object.

Fancy (stationery, stationary, stationiry) makes letter writing more enjoyable.

Go (strait, straight, strate) for two blocks, then turn left.

The (Strate, Strait) of Gibraltar is not very wide.

(Strenth, Strength, Stranth) is achieved by proper diet.

It was a (substantial, substancial, substantiel) settlement from their estate.

Being (suttle, subtle) can sometimes eliminate quarrels.

The three-room (suite, suit, sweet) was large enough for the two of us.

Plants can be damaged by the (son, sun) when there is no rain.

(Suppose, Suppos, Supose) we try the alternate method.

(Surprice, Surprise, Serprise)! Happy Anniversary!

Mystery writers must create (suspence, suspense, suspinse) for their readers.

The pudding was too (sweet, suite) for our visitor from Ohio.

An identifying (simble, symbol, cymbal) for a business is called a logo.

Empty is (synonomous, synonymous, sinonymus) with void.

A dog's (tale, tail) may be thin as a pencil or full and bushy.

Kevin told the assembled group a tall (tail, tale) which few believed.

The ship's (tair, tare, tear) had been miscalculated.

There was a long (tare, tair, tear) in his right sleeve.

A (tear, tier, teer) fell from her eye when she found her pet.

Alice had a (tendency, tendancy, tendensy) toward winking.

I like sugar more (then, than) any other sweetener.

(There, Their, They're) new car was badly scratched the day they bought it.

Ben and Jake only think of (themselves, themselfs).

We ate, (than, then) we went to the theatre in a taxicab to arrive early for the show.

Let's all go (they're, their, there) before they close.

Lillie and Debra called to say (their, they're, there) going to be late.

Do a (through, thorough, thurough) job and your boss will be pleased.

(Those, Thos, Thows) lamps do not belong in this display.

Lana (thought, thaught, thawt) she'd be selected Queen of the Fair.

Timmie (through, threw) the ball and his little dog chased it.

Pass the food (threw, through) the kitchen window, when it's ready.

Change the decoration on the third (tier, tear, teer) of the wedding cake.

(Too, To, Two) reach one's goal requires perseverance.

(Together, Togither) we will conquer the pesky weed problem.

(Two, Too, To) many people spell this easy word incorrectly.

Suddenly, the race became a (trajedy, tragidy, tragedy).

When Al was promoted, he was (transfered, transferred, transfirred) from one camp to another.

Helene (tried, tryed) to dance to the music on her ice skates.

A gardener (trys, tries) to grow beautiful flowers.

(Too, To, Two) or more runners are required for a relay race.

(Undoubtedly, Undoutidly, Undoutly), the car will run out of gas before they reach home.

A good carpenter will (yews, uce, use) the right tool for each task.

(Vacum, Vaccum, Vacuum) the living room first this time.

This (vue, view) from the bridge is spectacular.

Don't (wate, weight, wait) too long, dinner will get cold.

Some day we'll travel another (way, weigh, whey).

A model must (where, wear, ware) what is selected for her.

Willie, the (weather, whether, wether) man, had good news.

I'd very much like to (way, weigh) less than I do now.

That package's (wait, weight, wate) is much too high.

A (wierd, weird, weerd) note came in today's mail.

(Wear, Where, Ware) did the lovely flowers come from?

Billy liked the bike (weather, wether, whether) it was blue or not.

(Whose, Who's) invited to your Sweet Sixteen party?

The neighbor's dog ate the (hole, whole) roast alone.

(Who's, Whose) house is that across the street?

Gregory spoke to the (women, woman, womin) about cutting her lawn on a regular schedule.

Last week, I (one, won) first place in the tennis tournament.

A (right, wright) is a constructive workman, possibly a carpenter.

(Right, Write, Rite, Wright) to me each week when you're away.

(Use, Yews) are a decorative shrub for the front of a house.

Our enemy wouldn't (yield, yeild, yeeld) ground to our troops.

In days of (your, you're, yore), wardrobes were very different.

Is that (yore, your, you're) only reason for stopping?

I don't care if (your, you're, yore) late; the work must be completed.

Test Yourself Answers

p. 69   accommodate, accustom, achieve, acquaint, acquaintance, acquire, actual, advice, advise, affect, against, aisle, a lot, among, amount, analysis, analyze, answer, apparent, appreciate, approach

p. 70   approximate, arthritis, article, ate, athlete, bare, bear, beer, bier, blew, blue, board, bored, bouillon, brake, bread, break, bred, bullion, business, busy, canvas, canvass, careful, careless, category, cede, cent

p. 71   cents, certain, chief, choice, choose, chose, cite, clothes, comparative, condemn, conscience, conscientious, conscious, consider, continuous, convenience, criticism, criticize, curiosity, curious, curriculum, cymbal, dealt, dear

p. 72   deer, dependent, desert, desirability, desire, despair, dessert, difference, different, disappoint, disastrous, discipline, disease, divine, effect, efficient, eight, embarrass, equipment, equipped, especially, exaggerate

p. 73   excellence, excellent, excitable, exercise, expense, experience, experiment, explanation, extremely, fair, fare, fare, fascinate, favorite, faze, feat, feet, fictitious, field, flew, flue, for, fore, foreign

p. 74   forth, forty, forward, four, fourth, friend, fulfill, fundamental, gnu, grammar, grate, great, guarantee, guidance, guiding, hay, hear, height, here, hey, hole

p. 75   hors d'oeuvres, hour, huge, hungry, ignorance, I'll, indispensable, influential, interest, interfere, interpret, interpretation, interrupt, irrelevant, isle, it's, its, knew, know, knowledge, labor, laboratory, laborer, laid, later

p. 76   lead, lead, led, leisure, length, lengthening, liaison, license, likeness, logistics, loose, looser, lose, loser, luxury, made, maid, mail, maintenance, male, maneuver, marriage, mathematics

p. 77   meant, meat, mechanics, medicine, meet, meet, mete, miniature, mischief, narrative, necessary,

new, ninety, no, noticeable, noticing, obstacle, occur, occurred, occurrence, occurring

p. 78   omit, one, operate, opponent, oppose, optimism,
origin, original, our, pair, pail, pale, parallel, pare,
passed, past, peace, pear, perceive, permanent, persistent, personal, personnel, persuade, pertain

p. 79   phase, philosophy, physical, piece, playwright,
poinsettia, pore, pour, precede, prefer, preferred,
prejudice, pricing, primitive, principal, principle,
privilege, procedure, proceed

p. 80   prominent, psychology, pursue, quantity, rain, read,
read, real, receive, receiving, red, reed, reel, referring, reign, relative, relieve, religion, remember,
reminisce, represent

p. 81   rhythm, right, rite, road, rode, roe, root, route, row,
safety, scene, scent, schedule, science, sea, seam,
see, seed, seem, seen, seize, sense, sent, separate,
sergeant

p. 82   several, sew, shepherd, shoe, shoo, sight, sign, sine,
site, so, sold, soled, son, sophomore, source, speech,
sponsor, stationary, stationery, straight, strait,
strength, substantial, subtle, suite

p. 83   sun, suppose, surprise, suspense, sweet, symbol,
synonymous, tail, tale, tare, tear, tear, tendency,
than, their, themselves, then, there, they're, thorough, those, thought

p. 84   threw, through, tier, to, together, too, tragedy, transferred, tried, tries, two, undoubtedly, use, vacuum,
view, wait, way, wear, weather, weigh, weight,
weird, where, whether

p. 85   who's, whole, whose, woman, won, wright, write,
yews, yield, yore, your, you're

Proofreading and Copyediting Symbols

Symbols		Meanings
e	To get/ this color, I	Delete, take out that which is indicated
stet	One Saturday, ~~near~~ the	Stet, do not change what is underlined with dots
⊙	She called for help⊙	Change to a period
tr.	It w(sa) very late.	Transpose letters as indicated
/, or ⋀	At that moment⋀he	Insert comma where indicated
⋁	⋀Look!⋀she called out.	Insert quotation marks as indicated
:/ or ⋀	Dear Mr. Kelly⋀	Insert colon where indicated
;/ or ⋀	It was early⋀the new day was dawning.	Insert semi-colon where indicated
sp. out	The (R. C.) had come to the rescue.	Spell out, do not abbreviate
⊙	Turn the ca(n)oe around.	Turn letter right side up
=/	The once⋀radiant sky was now turning black.	Hyphenate as indicated

Symbols	**Meanings**
caps The Haunted House is the title.	Set in caps (capital letters)
s.c. Sports Titles	Set in small caps (reduced size)
l.c Susan ¢ame home this week.	Set in lower case (not capital letters, use small letters)
wf. Let's go to the right.	Wrong font (letters from different style type), change to correct style
ital. The witch was coming.	Set in italics
bf. POISON! DANGER TO YOUR HEALTH	Set in bold face (heavier letters)
× A short time later the fire was out.	Change damaged letter(s)
⊐]On May 24th, we left on a trip.	Move to right
⊏ [There is nothing more to say.	Move to left
m School was closed for the summer.	Change incorrect letter to letter in margin
eq # During the evening, we ∧ watched the sunset.	Change to equal spacing where indicated
out, *see copy* The man was hired because he∧a well-known university.	Out, see original copy (insert whatever is missing in space indicated)

Symbols	Meanings
# She‿worked for the company many years.	Insert space where indicated
= Every morning <u>they go for</u> a walk.	Level line of letters
◯ It was really a c͡ontagious disease.	Close up space
¶ Vacations are usually a special treat.¶ I like to	Start a new paragraph
⁓ ¶ at the dock.͝ ͟Gregory discovered he was interested in boating.	No paragraph here
ᣗ The book‿s cover was an eye-catcher.	Insert apostrophe as indicated